FIELD, FORM, AND FATE

FIELD, FORM, AND FATE

Patterns in Mind, Nature, and Psyche

MICHAEL CONFORTI

Spring Journal Books
New Orleans, Louisiana

Assisi Series 1

Published by
Spring Journal, Inc.;
627 Ursulines Street;
New Orleans, Louisiana 70116

Printed in Canada.
Text printed on acidfree paper.

Cover design by
Northern Cartographic
4050 Williston Road
South Burlington, VT 05403

Library in Congress Cataloging in Publication Data
Pending

DEDICATION

Vorrei dedicare questo libro al mio figlio, Cristoforo, all memo-ria della mia madre, Maria, al mio padre, Giovanni. Vi Voglio bene.

I would like to dedicate this book to my son, Christopher, to the memory of my mother, Maria, and to my father, John. I love you all very much.

Acknowledgments

The ideas and the spirit behind this book have been gestating for more than fifteen years, coinciding with the birth of the Assisi conferences in Assisi, Italy. In fact, even before the first conference, I had the good fortune to have found a mentor whose ideas and understanding of my psyche laid the groundwork for much of what was to evolve and continues to develop in my life. In the deepest sense of the word, he is my compadre or as we say in our Brooklyn-Sicilian dialect—guumbuh! I owe the deepest gratitude, appreciation and love to Yoram Kaufmann who has provided me with more than he or I may ever realize. I only hope that I can someday give as much back to him and to my own students.

There are a number of colleagues who have played a pivotal role in the development of the ideas within this book. These include: Fred Abraham, Lenore Thomson-Bentz, Mae Wan Ho, Mario Jacoby, Rise Kaufmann, Ervin Laszlo, F. David Peat, Beverly Rubik, Peter Saunders, Mara Sidoli, and my friend Dr. Rick Van der Poll affectionately referred to as Rick, the Mushroom man!

I also want to acknowledge the work of a number of innovative investigators of the psyche, who laid the groundwork for our ongoing understanding of the confluence of psyche and matter. These include: C. G. Jung, Zerka Moreno, Elizabeth Osterman, Ernest Rossi, Marie-Louise von Franz, and a great friend and colleague, Aryeh Maidenbaum. To Dr. Robert Langs, I want to say thank you for all the support and learning I have received from you over the years. Dr. Langs is a man with a pioneering vision, who has the courage to see things and to say things about human nature that many of us are afraid to. Thank you.

ACKNOWLEDGMENTS

There are many people within the Assisi Community who have brought much richness to this work. A warm and deep appreciation to John Finneran, Jyoti Jayaraman, Marianne Stigum, and Diane Antczak for all of their work in helping to make the Assisi Foundation and our Two-Year Training program such a vital and thriving reality.

As these ideas are now finding a warm reception and increased applications within the organizational domain, I want to thank the following for their support and intuitive understanding of the role of archetypal patterns in organizational life: Peter Burmeister, John Duncan, Sharon Matthias, Gary McPherson, Carol Pearson, Ivy Ross, and Phyllis Wooley-Fisher.

I want to thank all the friends who support this work in the Portland, Oregon Jungian community. I especially want to thank the members of my ongoing Portland seminar and the special efforts of Lola Bessey, Martha Blake, Larry and Elizabeth Kirkhardt, Jolinda Osborne, Shannon Pernetti, Gregg Smith, and The Oregon Friends of Jung Society.

I received invaluable assistance with the draft version of this material from my friends and colleagues, Michele Fogg, Judith Rossi, Nancy Stefanik, and Dr. Richard Ott, whose depth of knowledge has spirited much of this work.

A special thank you goes to the three women who graciously run the Country House, the home for our annual Assisi, Italy Conference, in Assisi. Sylvania, Luigia, and Susanna continue to provide so much warmth, comfort, and acceptance to our group. We have truly found a home at the Country House. Their love and care provides us with a wonderful place within which to return each year to do our work.

When originally presented for publication, this book was divided into two separate books. Mike Allison worked his magic with this manuscript and made it publishable. The idea for this revised edition came from Nancy Cater and Jay Livernois, the editors and owners of Spring Journal. Nancy spent hours fine-tuning this material and brought her gift of language and deep understanding of psyche to this editorial project. In so many ways, she has softened many of the rough edges

ACKNOWLEDGMENTS

in these ideas. I have a deep respect and fondness for Nancy and her work with Spring Journal. Thank you so much.

To Denise Bonello, our Program Director for the Assisi Conferences, thank you from the bottom of my heart for seamlessly attending to so many areas of my life. I have to admit that it's especially nice to have another New York Italian to work with, who understands my ways of doing things!

In many respects this revised edition reflects important changes in my own life. Clearly, the ongoing work with colleagues is essential. However, on a more personal note I want to thank Melisa DiBernardo for all she has brought into my life.

Contents

Foreword

From 1964-1968 I was a student at St. Francis Preparatory High School in Brooklyn, New York. There I passed many hours enthralled by stories of St. Francis' life and work, struck by his struggle to integrate the worlds of spirit and matter.

In 1989, now a Jungian analyst, lecturer, and teacher, I founded the Assisi, Italy Conference and have convened it for the past ten years. This interdisciplinary program investigates the interface between Jungian psychology and the new sciences with an emphasis on the archetypal dimensions of self-organization.

There, amid the beauty of the Umbrian countryside that inspired St. Francis, I find myself seeking the confluence of matter, psyche, and spirit as St. Francis sought to do more than seven centuries ago. Why Assisi, and why pursue in a seemingly fated manner St. Francis' vision of matter and psyche? Perhaps as this book unfolds, the reader will see that life is as often silently guided by the presence and influence of an archetype as it is by personal choice. In fact C. G. Jung found that archetypes are responsible for the high degree of self-organization found in both the human psyche and natural world.

So, is this ongoing concern and interest in what St. Francis viewed as matter-spirit concerns simply a coincidence or evidence of the overarching power of archetypes? I trust that Jung and many other investigators in the area of mind/matter and consciousness studies would speak of a fated and purposeful nature to this attraction. Perhaps this represents an unfolding of a richly textured destiny. May time and wisdom tell.

Introduction to First Edition

This book, *Field, Form, and Fate: Patterns in Mind, Nature, and Psyche,* draws on findings from the sciences and the work of C. G. Jung to discuss the archetypal dynamics of self-organization as it applies to the individual psyche and the natural world. My position is that Jung's theory of the archetype is the psychological parallel to the scientific theory of self-organizing dynamics in nature.

Jung believed that the human psyche inherits its ways of formulating information and relating to it by way of unconscious blueprints called "archetypes." He compared the archetype to the axial system of a crystal, which determines the crystalline structure in the mother liquid, although it has no material existence of its own. In the same way, the archetype is purely formal. Its impetus, according to Jung, is similar to that of the instincts. Ervin Laszlo, a dynamical systems theorist and pioneer in the new sciences, describes the same kind of dynamics at work in nature: "Fields predate the configuration of matter and . . . matter emerges out of these prefigured informational fields." *Field, Form, and Fate* seeks to comprehend the human psyche as part of the larger natural order in which the archetypes are continually becoming incarnate in space and time.

One can infer an archetypal order even at the most basic level of human incarnation—the fetus in the womb. The form a baby eventually develops may be said to exist even prior to the act of conception. Although classical biologists have attributed the appearance and development of form to the unfolding of the DNA process, there is no evidence of any chemical blueprint located in the DNA code which can account for the specificity of form. Thus a number of contemporary researchers have turned to the idea of "fields" to explain the constancy and stability of particular forms over time. This book discusses some of the current debates occurring in Jungian psychology, biology, physics, archetypal psychology, bioelectro-dynamics, and general principles of self-organization.

Specifically I will focus on the way in which the development of form invariably proceeds from the simple to the complex. For example, in the earliest stages of human life, development occurs by way of replication. The original cell simply reproduces and splits off from itself. It is only after this replicative regime is stabilized that we find the emergence of diversity and complexity.

In employing the psychotherapeutic situation as a primary illustration of this dynamic in human terms, I suggest that the form taken by a therapeutic relationship in its early stages is created by a replication of dynamics found in the respective psyches of the client and therapist. The interactional resonance and entrainment that develops as a result not only underlies the peculiar sense of rapport that occurs in the therapeutic dyad—as well as in all relationships known to the material world, by extension—but also makes possible the more mysterious aspects of the relationship: the synchronization and entrainment of psyches, synchronistic events and parallel thought processes rarely discussed outside the fields of particle physics, biophysics, and parapsychology.

The dynamics and interactions occurring in therapy may, in this respect, be understood as "field-produced-phenomena." They represent archetypal potential manifesting in space and time. Knowledge of the specific archetype generating the field can be inferred from the typical constellation of psychic phenomena around its structure. Numerous examples from the clinical domain as well as from the outer world are included in this book.

In fact much of the book is concerned with what I call an "archetypal field theory," or a "confluence theory," as well as archetypal pattern recognition. The latter involves the work of recognizing the symbolic expressions of particular archetypes and the specific life tasks involved in addressing their themes. Examples from biology and the natural world are included to highlight the importance of these processes, as well as to introduce current methodologies in the area of pattern recognition.

In addition to drawing on Jung's perspectives on the psyche's natural tendency toward self-organization and self regulation, and his theory of the archetype, this book synthesizes the ideas of pioneers in related disciplines, many of whom I am fortunate to consider colleagues. Included are Ervin Laszlo's work on the Psi and vacuum field, Rupert Sheldrake's theory of morphic resonance and formative causation, F. David Peat's work on the interrelationship between mind and matter, David Bohm's concept of the implicate order, and Brian Goodwin's and Mae-Wan Ho's work on morphogenetic processes in organisms and fields.

The book's subtitle suggests the need to reevaluate the growing emphasis on cognitive and constructionist theories of mind as ego-based, viewing postmodern reality as merely the product or construction of one's perceptions. Instead this book champions the autonomy of the psyche. Human perception and cognition represent important, albeit relatively small, slices of human experience. Self-organization occurs outside the domain of conscious perception and becomes available to conscious awareness only in retrospect on the basis of its results.

Field, Form, and Fate suggests that apparent human distinctions are contained within a larger dimension of meaning. This perspective has opened the door for speculation into both human discord and strategies of intervention and resolution, along the lines of the Club of Budapest's research project, "Promoting Planetary Peace," of which I have had the honor of being an invited participant. Is this just a coincidence? I wonder if Jung or St. Francis of Assisi would think so. I know what I have experienced.

Michael Conforti
February 14, 1999
Brattleboro, Vermont

Introduction to Revised Edition

Since childhood, the subtle expressions of human nature and the beauties of the natural world have emotionally touched me. There was always a juxtaposition between the cruelty and violence in the world and the grandeur found in nature. Growing up in Brooklyn we never saw much of nature except when we went to the local balls fields for baseball games. Prospect Park and The Parade Grounds were a haven for us city kids wanting to feel a little grass under our feet. However, we quickly learned that nature was not only experienced through the out of doors, but also came through in other, equally dramatic ways. The essence of one's own nature is just as important. Language and tradition provide significant ways to learn about one's archetypal and cultural nature.

As a child, I was immersed in a big Italian family. My father's side of the family, the Confortis, were from Sicily and Calabria, while my mother's side, the D'Amatos and the Ferninos, immigrated from Salerno, a southern Italian town near Naples.

My early experience of cultural diversity was heightened by the fact that from six months of age until I was nearly two, I spent virtually every day with my father's sisters and parents, while my mother had to work to help support our family. From infancy, I was immersed in the Sicilian culture, and to this day the song-like sounds of that dialect, the aromas of Sicilian foods, and the cultural values inherent in the Sicilian Psyche continue to permeate my soul and are obvious in my behaviors.

These impressions continue to influence my daily life. I was born in a multicultural environment. Here I was living in Brooklyn, in a predominantly Italian neighborhood, with a plethora of other cultures thriving within a few blocks of our little enclave. My daily trips to school traversed multiple worlds. Traveling from Bensenhurst to Holy Cross Grammar School in Flatbush, the bus would begin the trek in the Italian neighborhood, go on to the strangely mysterious Hasidic section, then enter the area where the Greek immigrants and their families settled, and finally end this cultural odyssey on Flatbush Avenue, a melting pot of cultures. With these daily excursions, I was brought into the domains of many worlds with many different languages, traditions, foods, and cultures. While all were connected by the common thread we all share as humans, one had to only open his senses and taste buds to be affected by the traditions of these different cultural groups.

In giving the opening address at a recent Assisi, Italy Conference, I spoke of my early immersions into "different worlds" and how my sense of multiple worlds continues to this day. The very nature of my work and the ideas in this book express a lifelong sense that the manifest, material world we see around us is but a part of a much larger, more intricate, more interesting and, yes, much more powerful world. We can see how the world of the ego and its values, tendencies, and interests pale in comparison to the will and demands of the Self. The Swiss psychoanalyst C.G. Jung spent his entire life's work mapping out the contours of this other world. For Jung, and for the past twenty-five years of my own work on the primacy of the archetype, the innate ordering processes in the psyche have remained the central focus.

Tremendous efforts abound to solidify the ego's (not the Self's) position as the central player in the drama of life. Entire schools of thought are built around this premise. The theories of Subjectivity and Constructionism are but two that attempt to diminish the importance of the objective psyche. Each searches for truth and ultimate meaning in the individual's personal, subjective reactions, all part of a trend that I call "personal, subjective relativism." Many modern Jungians have also shifted their orientation away from the nature of the objective psyche and its archetypes to focus on the subjective reactions of their clients. For instance, in the clinical use of dreams, we all too often seek the meaning of an image by eliciting the client's and therapist's thoughts and feelings about it. The frame of reference is drawn from the limited personal experiences of both parties. "I think this" and "you think that" become the basis of the interpretation.

As an illustration, let's say someone dreams of a taking a July summer vacation in Florida and reveling in watching turtles hatching on the beach.[1] Client and therapist may easily assume that the image reveals something about new life coming to fruition, and with this discovery, both feel self-congratulatory about the success of the therapy. However, we find a very different story and meaning emerging when we look at the image from the perspective of the innate tendencies and habits of turtles in the natural world. While the subjective interpretation is useful in determining the individual's alignment to the archetype, it will not necessarily reveal anything about the archetype itself.

So how do we move beyond our own conscious orientation to learn something about the non-personally derived, innate dimension of the image? One useful way is to consult a specialist or book to discover highly specific information about the particular image. With this turtle-hatching image, we find, after consulting a specialist in turtle behavior, that turtles *will not hatch* during the summer, as the intensity of the Florida sunshine will burn and damage the precious life contained within the shell. In addition, we find that only 1 out of 10,000 baby turtles ever make it to maturity. So suddenly, we have a much richer, broader, and more truthful rendering of the image, which dramatically expands our conscious appreciation and understanding of it. With this information we move from a hopeful, rejoicing rending of the dream to a position that suggests that something is attempting to come to fruition at a time that will almost certainly result in death. Additionally, we find that the survival rate of turtles is so low that even under the best of circumstances, the birth process will still occur under conditions of great adversity.

---

1. Thanks to colleague Jane Carr for sharing this dream with me.

As we move beyond our own subjective context and approach the archetypal domain, we need to recognize the limited range of knowledge contained within our personal unconscious. When we look at the nature of archetypal images, we begin a process which is essentially spiritual, in that it respects a position outside of conscious knowledge and awareness. In our prayers and meditations we also work to quiet the noise of our daily conscious rumblings in order to allow for something greater and more compelling to enter our lives.

While obviously valuing the importance of subjective reactions, Jung stressed the superordinate role of the objective psyche in human affairs. I will never forget an event that points to the tremendous dangers inherent in a subjectively based approach to life and phenomena. While participating in doctoral students' oral exams, we listened to a clinical presentation about a female patient who from childhood on experienced some of the greatest tragedies I had ever heard of. One of these tragedies occurred during her teenage years, when she was participating in a pep rally. In an attempt to hype up the sporting event, the driver of the truck on which she and one of her girlfriends were riding decided to speed up over some railroad tracks. Losing their balance, both girls fell off the truck, and the leg of the patient's friend was severed when she landed on a barbed wire fence.

We asked the doctoral student how he and his client worked with this story in the treatment. The student-therapist explained that he asked the patient how *she viewed the event.* She spoke of being spared by God and, on the other hand, of how this event must be God's way of punishing her for something she did wrong. My colleague, a clinical and research psychologist who was a bright and reasonable man, joined in the discussion, suggesting that the client could have found the accident interesting, in that with the severed body parts one could clearly see the veins, muscles, tendons, etc. Yes, he went on, this could have been a real learning experience. I just couldn't take any more and said "you are both crazy-pazzo!" To spin these fantastic, whimsical, and, yes, I will say even psychotic, manic renderings of such a hideous event is inane and speaks more to a shared denial of the objective sense of horror that *had to be the most truthful* rendering of the event. While this is clearly a dramatic story, it captures the dangers inherent in totemizing the ego, an attitude and approach rampant in modern culture.

Life is *not only what we make it.* Life happens, and in more instances than not, our work is to respond to these archetypal influences, which are far greater and predate the formation of human consciousness and will. We only have to look around us to see examples of the independent properties of psyche and nature. The entire field of Feng Shui tells us how space and the actual location of a room or a restaurant will inevitably affect us whether or not we are consciously aware of it. Also, the mysteriously beautiful formations found in nature, like those in seashells, animal designs, etc., all attest to the knowledge and innate design contained in the natural world.

Perhaps the deepest, archetypal issue embedded in the relationship between the personal and the objective involves our relationship with the divine. In a brilliant and touching article, entitled "The Periplus of the Eranos Archetype," (2003), Rudolf Ritsema, Director of the Eranos Conferences, offers a thoughtful perspective on the relationship between personal and objective, archetypal emotions. He writes:

> The Greek language has various terms to denote love. Eros and philo refer to love with a subject and object, a love that is a personal involvement and usually expects something in return (gratitude if nothing else!)— Whereas agape indicates love without any specific focus, an overflowing fullness of the heart, which cannot but be shared with whomever comes in contact with it, without expecting anything in return.... (3-4)

Living solely within the personal domain, (*Eros* and *philo*), we end up recycling all too familiar information and material. However, touching the transpersonal (*agape*) creates an opening into something much greater than oneself. Mystics, poetics, philosophers, musicians, and individuals in love have all commented on this sense of oneness with the world and with the origins of creative expression. I'm really not so sure if any creative act can emerge without a dipping into this archetypal domain. The objective psyche, like nature, will create powerful reactions to the pushes and pulls of will and our attempts to shift archetypal reality into what *we want it* to be. Our knowledge of the natural world and our continuing advances in technology must work hand in hand with nature. Despite our efforts to manipulate and craft nature according to our will, its own ways will still be heard. The city of Venice is but one of any number of examples of this nature-technology issue. Ever increasingly complex plans are made to curb the flooding of this remarkable city, yet the waters and floods march on with the cyclicity of the coming of the seasons. The strength of these natural processes will prevail and will never be fully silenced.

Discussion of the innate wisdom of the psyche and nature also takes us into the exciting world of the new sciences of complexity and emergence. This work speaks about the generation of form, the field from which manifestations of form arise, and those processes responsible for the emergence of order in the world. The early alchemists understood the intrinsic relationship between the natural world of matter and the domain of the spirit and psyche. Considered the precursor to modern chemistry, alchemy saw in the manifestation of dense matter incarnations of the divine. Goethe's interest in "all that is destined to become manifest" (quoted in Portmann, *New Paths,* 76) led to an intuition about a divinely appointed, universal blueprint upon which all form is configured.

Adolf Portmann, the noted biologist, colleague of C. G. Jung, and long-time contributor to the Eranos Conferences, was perhaps one of the most elegant speakers on this confluence. The prevailing scientific paradigm in Portmann's day, which continues to influence current scientific inquiry, looked at biological form and behavior strictly in terms of its role in ensuring survival. Portmann, however, posited a revolutionary position. His work draws upon the many instances of ornamentation in animals, such as colors of feathers, etc., which have little, if any, survival value. Portmann suggests that the imperative to express one's intrinsic nature, as seen in decorative ornamentation, is perhaps even more important than the need for self-preservation. So the mandate for virtually all-living systems, according to Portmann, is twofold: to insure survival and to express one's nature. He thus speaks of bird songs as a decorative expression of a bird's innate identity. In the following, we glimpse Portmann's unique vision:

> The most modest plant... expresses its independent being in the form of its leaf, flower, and fruit, as does the butterfly in its larva, pupa and imago. Those marine snails which are seen by no eye except that of the occasional human explorer, express their essence in a host of splendid forms and colors—each according to its kind. Their appearance speaks a language of which we suspect we can grasp a few words, and gives evidence of a hidden power of life, that goes beyond the needs of self-preservation. (*New Paths*, 159)

Portmann's focus on material form as expressive of the field from which it is generated speaks to the perennial notion of an *Unus Mundus* —a one world. Einstein longed to find a unified view of the world, a theory that could collapse the ideas of different fields into one unified field. The notion of a superstring theory also hoped to collapse various fields into a singular field. Akin to plucking a guitar string at different points and at various frequencies to produce different notes, the superstring theory views the electromagnetic field, gravitational field, etc. as different notes on the same string.

It is but a short step to see how the work on unified fields has stirred our interests in body-mind issues and encouraged a revisioning of the entire field of psychosomatic medicine. The distinctions between mind and body and psyche and matter can be put to rest, as we more fully understand that each is an expression and explication of the other. In this light, we find David Bohm's work on the implicate order particularly compelling. Bohm sees the implicate order as the matrix out of which everything arises. From musical and artistic inspiration, to innate ordering principles, to the generation of form, Bohm sees each as an expression of an implicate, archetypal field, finding a corresponding means of expression in the outer world. Here we find a fascinating confluence of ideas between the work of Jung, who posits the *a priori* existence of the archetype and its symbolic expression, Laszlo's idea of the *vacuum plenum*, (previously his PSI field theory) as the creative matrix for life, Rupert Sheldrake's view of form as expressive of formative, morphogenetic fields, and even the Bible, where we find the word made flesh. Each speaks to an *a priori* field, where form, living *in potentia*, is converted into matter. On some level there is no form without its generative field and no field without its corresponding form.

To make yet one more extension of the implication of these ideas of a unified field, where form is expressive of the field from which it originates, we can begin to shift yet another bastion of modern consciousness, namely the notion of pathology. Traditionally, pathology is viewed as any behavior deviating from the norm. From Freud's early work on sexuality to prevailing views on mental health and medical research, pathology expresses something that has gone wrong. We rarely grasp the enormity of this concept and its impact on our lives, nor do we realize how in designating behavior as pathological, we fail to understand how psyche expresses itself in often mysterious, baffling, and, at times, disturbing ways.

If we follow the thread from alchemy to Jung's work on the objective psyche and on to the new sciences, we stand in an excellent position from which to shift the paradigm from pathology to expression. In this light, we begin to appreciate every configuration in the individual and natural world as an expression of an underlying order. While this order may not be generative, it is nevertheless highly patterned and archetypally influenced.

Consider for instance the situation of a depressed child. One could do a lot of fancy therapeutic footwork focused on behavior to help him become a happier, better adjusted child. The work would be aimed at changing what is assumed to be highly dysfunctional behavior—the depression—to something more positive. We could work to determine the cause of the depression and perhaps even recommend anti-depressant drugs. Now if we shift the picture from one of pathology and dysfunction to one of expression, we may find the child's behavior governed by a potentially generative, goal-directed force. As we further shift this old paradigm, we look at the nature of the developing configuration and not at what has gone wrong. Remember the adage that every picture tells a story. Well, with the shift I am suggesting, we turn this saying around and find that *every story has a picture.* The theoretical inference here refers to the overarching, *a priori* field, which finds a correspondence in symbolic and behavioral manifestations. Here, form reveals as much about the nature of the image itself as it does about the field from which it has emerged. Goodwin and Sole (2000), in *Signs of Life: How Complexity Pervades Biology,* make a similar point when writing:

> The concept of emergence, once regarded by many biologists as a vague and mystical concept with dangerous vitalist connotations, is now the central focus of the sciences of complexity. Here the question is, how can systems made up of components whose properties we understand give rise to phenomena that are quite unexpected? Life is the most dramatic manifestation of this process, the domain of emergence par excellence. But the new sciences unite biology with physics in a manner that allows us to see the creative fabric process as a single dynamic unfolding. (x)

In order to help this child and to understand the nature and goal of his depression, we have to wonder where, if left to *its own accord,* this drama it will lead. Borrowing from Bohm's "Ontological Approach" in understanding phenomena, one may merely comment on the essence of the situation itself, saying something to the effect of "It is striking that you have little interest in the activities *around you.*" While deceptively simple, this interventional approach strives to understand the pattern in its own right, free from one's particular biases. Similar to Kaufmann's (1996) "orientational approach," this method works to articulate the intrinsic, symbolic nature of the emergent situation.

In this case, I focused on the lack of energy-libido invested in the depressed child's daily activities. From these discussions, it was clear that he was depressed because he was continually encouraged by his family and peers to participate in the more typical childhood activities, such as sports, cub scouts, outings, etc., whereas he desperately longed for a more active engagement in the arts, including theatre and music. In addition, as depression refers to a withdrawal and pulling in of energy, we can also say that his creative energy and élan vital remained in his interior life, perhaps waiting and hoping for the time when his true nature would find fertile ground. As his life was being channeled into a domain incongruous with his nature, his depression was perfectly understandable. To treat the depression as an illness would have been a terrible mistake, and in so doing, his deepest needs would not have been met.

I hope this new introduction presents my continuing thoughts on the nature of archetypes, their emergence into matter, and the patterns they form. To capture the direction indicated by psyche brings us in line with our own destiny. Destiny appears to be inborn and unfolds in the course of one's life. To live one's destiny is to be aligned with what is most generative in life. Not to do so creates a personal and collective misery and estrangement from one's soul. Archetypal manifestations call for human understanding and integration in order to bring these contents to consciousness. However, as Goethe suggests:

> So long as you don't live
> thus "Die and be transformed!"
> you will only be a gloomy guest
> on this dark earth.
> (*Selige Sehnsucht*, Stanley Appelbaum translation)

Michael Conforti
April 2003
Brattleboro, Vermont

CHAPTER ONE

Deja Vu All Over Again
Repetition in the Psyche and the Natural World

T he archetype, according to C. G. Jung (1875-1961), is a
preexistent, non-personally acquired informational field in
the collective unconscious. The archetypes themselves can
never be fully known or seen, but only gleaned from their incarnations as symbols and images, in situations, and through synchronicity,
etc. In much the same manner as the instinct is an inherent feature of
the human psyche, so too, Jung believed, is the archetype.

> [T]he instincts are not vague and indefinite by nature, but
> are specifically formed motive forces which, long before
> there is any consciousness, and in spite of any degree of
> consciousness later on, pursue their inherent goals. Conse-
> quently they form very close analogies to the archetypes,
> so close in fact that there is good reason for supposing that
> the archetypes are the unconscious images of the instincts
> themselves, in other words, they are *patterns of instinctual
> behavior. (CW 9i, § 91)

The relationships among instincts, archetypes, and patterns are
important to any investigation involving the emergence of form. The
instinct carries with it an imperative that compels the individual
and group within its influence to action, as a motive force to be fol-
lowed. Both in the biologically driven instincts—such as the need to
eat, drink, and sleep—or in the psychobiologically/archetypally
derived instinctive patterns—such as the need to couple, to relate,
and to retaliate—we see the life process continually directed by

instinctive forces. As we consider the tenacity with which instincts elicit a response and call for satiation, we see that their content carries material essential for survival.

Jung described an instinct as the physical manifestation of an archetypal process, having found form in matter. For instance, the sexual drive is a temporal, physicalized representation of the archetype of union, or *coniunctio*, and related to it are a series of specific symbols, images, and behaviors that are also expressed physically and temporally. While there are many personal variations and subjective meanings of sexuality, this archetype conveys guidance vital to the continuation of life at the emotional, spiritual, and biological levels. The archetype, which Jung often described as the meaning dimension of the instinct, also conserves and disseminates information necessary for the successful evolution of the individual and the species.

Many have wondered about the origin of archetypal structures, and with this arises the question of where and how the original form for any structure evolves. This theme has been addressed from many fronts, including physics (Hawking, 1988); astrophysics (Mansfield, 1995; Peat, 1987, 1998; and Weinberg, 1978); systems theory (Laszlo, 1987, 1988, 1990, 1992, 1993, 1994, 1996 and Bateson, 1972, 1979); biology (Waddington, 1972; Goodwin, 1972, 1978, 1983, 1989; Sheldrake, 1981, 1984, 1988; Csanyi, 1989; Csanyi and Kampis, 1985, 1991); and biophysics (Mae-Wan Ho, 1993 and Beverly Rubik, 1992, 1996).

In 1938, Jung addressed the question of original form for archetypal structures:

> Whether this psychic structure and its elements, the archetypes, ever "originated" at all is a metaphysical question and therefore unanswerable. The structure is something given, the precondition that is found to be present in every case. (*CW 9i*, § 187)

While I agree with Jung that we may never fully understand how archetypal structures originated, examining how related disciplines in the new sciences investigate the emergence of form will hopefully lead us to a better understanding of archetypes and their own particular role in the generation of form. The need for such an interdisciplinary approach to psyche and human nature, which is employed throughout this book, is thoughtfully discussed by Edward 0. Wilson (1998) as consilience, which he describes as:

> a belief in the unity of the sciences—a conviction, far deeper than a mere working proposition, that the world is orderly and can be explained by a small number of natural laws ... In modern physics its focus has been the unification of all the forces of nature . . . (*Consilience*, 4)

Einstein makes a similar point when writing: "It is a wonderful feeling to recognize the unity of a complex of phenomena that to direct observation appear to be quite separate things." (qted in *Consilience,* 5)

Life for all species develops in response to a set of innate blueprints providing the opportunity for growth, development, and survival. While the conservative laws of nature serve to maintain original form and design, the conditions are also set for the creation of diversity. Each rose shares a common origin, yet is also unique.

The same processes influence human growth. We are conceived and develop in response to morphogenetic consistencies that can be viewed as genetically and archetypally determined. As the fetus grows in accordance with these consistencies and demonstrates a high degree of informational similarity with other human fetal forms, we see the strength of morphogenetic, repetitive patterns.

Rupert Sheldrake's work offers an interesting perspective on the nature of archetypal patterns. His theories of morphogenetic fields, formative causation, and morphic resonance present a quasibiological explanation for the conservation and transference of information into form. According to Sheldrake, memory is stored in what he terms "morphic fields." Classical biologists, on the other hand, believe that genetic coding and the unfolding of the informational contents of the DNA threads are the central factors in morphogenetic processes. Their approach, which is essentially reductive and mechanistic, constricts the understanding of form to its being purely a product of biological processes. Sheldrake speaks instead of information being embedded in non-spatio-temporal fields. For example, he posits that each acorn learns of its prospective evolutionary trajectories through its relationship to an oak tree morphic field in much the same manner as individuals have access to archetypal material.

Sheldrake accounts for the transmission of new information by suggesting that each time a new task for survival is learned, it is added to the cumulative store of material contained in the morphic field. What was initially a novel experience quickly becomes assimilated into the morphic field as memory and habit, thus becoming available to all members of the species. As new information finds its way into a field, its power to influence future forms is strengthened through habitual reiterations. These memory traces, or "chreodic patterns," comprise an informational pool constantly available to the group. They then influence the generation of future form within the field by releasing their informational contents.

Implied in Sheldrake's theory is the premise that each new form is more an expression of a morphic field being realized in matter than it is simply the unfolding of biological processes. In other words, Sheldrake's theory of evolutionary development posits that the emergence of form is driven primarily by the realization of archetypes and archetypal patterns into form. For this and other reasons, his position is keenly debated. However, as valuable as Sheldrake's position is for understanding how archetypal material may be stored and transmitted within a system, he tends to avoid the question of first, or original, form. Neglecting the larger question of *a priori,* form-influencing fields is reductionistic, though his work makes an important contribution to our understanding of the relationship between matter and psyche.

Brian Goodwin, a renowned developmental biologist and student of the late C. H. Waddington, presents an interesting critique of Sheldrake's work. He notes that Sheldrake views form as emerging in response to fields that exist external to the organism. Goodwin suggests that Sheldrake's hypothesis of an externally driven field acting on the species creates an unnecessary and false dualism between field and organism.

Goodwin believes that Sheldrake's position ignores the vitality of the organism itself and its own innate ability to create and generate form. In contrast, Goodwin emphasizes the field embedded and contained *within the organism itself*. He proposes a unitary position where the organism and its informational field are viewed as one and the same. His theory thus collapses the duality inherent in Sheldrake's hypothesis.

Goodwin awards a similar value to the integrity and intelligence of the organism as did his mentor C. H. Waddington, considered by many to be the most important figure in the world of embryology. F. David Peat, a noted physicist, describes Waddington's view of the unfolding of information from DNA strands. Waddington, according to Peat, believed that the release of information within the DNA structure was sequentially coded and refractory to the push and pull of temporal perturbations. While agitations might initially upset the sequencing of the expression of DNA material through processes Waddington termed canalization, it would quickly return to its original course and release the necessary information without damaging the organism or causing a mutation in the original morphogenetic plan.

Waddington's speculations about the capacity of the organism to absorb perturbations is borne out in the degree of reliability and constancy found in human and animal form. Robert Rosen makes a similar point in his discussion of the transmission of genetic information and its mathematical equivalent: "The mathematical properties ... are constrained by the biological prerequisites for the stability and accessibility of the (genetic) information." (Rosen, 317) The ideas of both Waddington and Rosen address the degree of constraint placed on a system's evolution and lead us to speculate about the consistency of form found in archetypal structures.

FIELD, FORM, AND FATE

Freud's Contribution to Our Understanding of the Role of Patterns and Repetition in Psyche and Nature

Freud, in *Beyond the Pleasure Principle* (1920), offers a fascinating, though self-contradictory picture of the repetition compulsion. He states that the desire to repeat inevitably brings with it a sense of distress and psychological upheaval, often results in a traumatic experience, and is carried out in opposition to the individual's drive to satisfy the pleasure principle. Struck by the seeming willfulness of the urge to repeat and its tendency to override so central a human need as pleasure, Freud struggled to uncover the origin of this drive and to examine its possible goal(s).

What is clear in Freud's work is his understanding of the compelling nature and inherent power in the compulsion to repeat.

> The manifestations of a compulsion to repeat . . . exhibit to a high degree an instinctual character, and when they act in opposition to the pleasure principle, give the appearance of some ... force at work. (*Beyond the Pleasure Principle*, 35)

What is especially interesting here is a comment by the editors of Freud's *Collected Works* who add in a footnote that the German word *trieb,* used by Freud and which we translate as "instinct," "bears much more of a feeling of urgency than the [meaning of the] English 'instinct.'" (*Beyond the Pleasure Principle*, 35) This reference points to Freud's growing realization that an autonomous force exists beyond the personal dimension of the repetition, which strives to achieve *its own goal* in much the same way as archetypes and instincts.

Freud's observation of the urgency to carry out the repetition led him to consider the existence of

> an organic compulsion to repeat [that] lie[s] in the phenomena of heredity and the facts of embryology. We see how the germ of a living animal is obliged in the course of its development to recapitulate . . . the structures of all the forms from which it sprung . . . . (*Beyond the Pleasure Principle,* 37)

6

Freud quickly realized the contradictory nature of his observations about the phenomenon of repetition. On the one hand, he saw the tendency to repeat as an attempt to avoid anxiety and internal distress. He explained that the repetition is enacted as a defense against remembering. If the traumatic event is externalized through some form of repetition, then the anxiety that will inevitably arise if the meaning of the event is considered and consciously examined is lessened. Freud thus theorized that repeating is a way to avoid remembering.

On the other hand, Freud understood that the repetition is also a natural event constantly occurring in the human and nonhuman domain that preserves form and shapes patterns. He hovered between a reductive, causal interpretation and an a-causal one, tending to emphasize the universality of the replicative mode and its relationship to time-worn habits of nature. Drawing from his observations of the natural world where replication is evident, he wrote that "we soon call to mind examples from animal life which seem to confirm the view that instincts are historically determined." (*Beyond the Pleasure Principle,* 36-37)

Freud cited the migratory flight of birds as well as the salmon's return to spawn in its place of birth as further evidence of the occurrence of repetition in the natural world. Interestingly enough, scientists have for years sought an explanation for the seemingly eternal, cyclical processes of migration. Current findings now suggest that migratory routes track a series of natural grid lines in the earth and sea and contain specific electromagnetic frequencies. Each migrating animal possesses a type of receiver mechanism, which tunes into these electromagnetic fields and navigates in accordance with them. These findings give yet further reason to consider that human life as well is lived in accordance with a pre-laid, archetypal grid, which may function to align each of us with an innate destiny factor. Here again we have reason to consider a much deeper confluence between matter and psyche than previously recognized.

Replicative behaviors demand an expenditure of tremendous amounts of energy and are usually carried out at the expense of individual life. They are apparently subsumed within an eternal drama that has as one of its goals, as in the case of salmon, a return to the source to accomplish renewal.

The dual nature of the repetition instinct is also reflected in Freud's theory of a life and death drive. In the personal domain, the repetition often leads the individual in the direction of abuse and into a non-generative adaptation toward life, all in the service of maintaining and subsidizing a stable alignment with a specific face of the archetype. In other words, the purposeful dimension of repetition is that it insures the stable and highly regulated unfolding of a preformed morphological regime. Still, Freud was also forced to see the complementary nature of the repetition drive that continually works to renew life. To further this point, he cites important discoveries in the biological sciences, noting:

> research [that] was directed to the experimental testing on unicellular organisms of the alleged immortality of living substances. An American biologist, Woodruff, experimenting with a ciliate infusorian, the "slipper-animalcule," which reproduces by fission into two individuals, persisted until the 3029th generation . . . . This remote descendent of the firs slipper-animalcule. . . was just as lively as its ancestor and showed no signs of ageing or degeneration. (*Beyond the Pleasure Principle,* 47)

Following up on Woodruff's work, scientists are now reporting the existence of a cell that defies the tendency to structurally degenerate and instead stays perpetually healthy by maintaining its ability to self-replicate.

When the Freudian perspective on the repetition compulsion is applied to the therapeutic situation, we find a tendency among clinicians to focus on its reductive, destructive, and regressive aspects, neglecting its forward-moving, life-preserving dimension. To a large degree, the majority of therapeutic paradigms see the compulsion to repeat as a reactivation of an infantile condition and treat it as further evidence of an arrested developmental state.

REPETITION IN THE PSYCHE AND THE NATURAL WORLD

After rereading Freud's *Remembering, Repeating and Working-Through* (1914), I realized how fully he viewed the repetition as an opportunity for the patient and therapist to understand their respective psyches because it created a form through which the underlying archetypal morphology could emerge. In this regard, replication is a representation and externalization of an internal, archetypal mapping that has found a corresponding mode of presentation in matter. The replication is thus informationally rich in that it conveys vital data about the individual's archetypal blueprint. However, many of Freud's successors misinterpreted his original and creative contributions to the phenomenon and settled on a reductive interpretation. Writing on the purposive nature of illness, in a passage that can be extended to the activation of the repetition, Freud states that the patient:

> must find the courage to direct his attention to the phenom-
> ena of his illness. His illness itself must no longer seem to
> him contemptible, but must become…worthy of his mettle,
> a piece of his personality, which has solid ground for its
> existence and out of which things of value for his future
> life have to be derived. (*Remembering, Repeating and
> Working-Through,* 152)

So too must the client and therapist adopt an investigative stance regarding the occurrence of the repetition. Instead of settling for an explanation that simply searches in the past for an answer to the current behavior, they need to ask to what end is the repetition geared. This results in an ontological, rather than pathological, approach to behavior, which may lead us to discover the deeper meaning embedded in the expression of the replication.

Freud also observed that the analytic process often begins with the patient repeating within the context of the patient-therapist relationship some version of his/her internal struggle.

> The greater the resistance, the more extensively will acting
> out (repetition) replace remembering . . . (*Remember-
> ing, Repeating and Working Through,* 151)

> [T]he patient does not *remember* anything of what he
> has forgotten and repressed, but *acts* it out. He repro-
> duces it not as a memory but as an action . . . .
> (*Remembering,* 150)

For Freud, the transference relationship established between
patient and therapist was the specific arena in which the strength of
the repetition was directly experienced. While we see the tendency
to repeat in virtually every facet of human life, the therapeutic situation is embedded within an archetypal field carrying with it its own
influences and tendencies, one of which is that it proceeds along replicative lines forward, hopefully toward greater complexity. As is well
known of the classic analytic method, the very occurrence of the repetition is a pivotal element in the therapeutic process and, if understood,
is invaluable in helping in the individual's recovery. Replication also
aids in the healing process by presenting a clear representation and
manifestation of a constellated archetypal alignment, which becomes
visible in the entrainment established in the therapeutic dyad. Consequently, replications are informative and revealing of both the
personal past and the archetypal dominants of one's life.

Theodore Reik's View of the Repetition

Theodore Reik's work is an important addition to our understanding of the repetition compulsion. In his seminal book,
Listening with the Third Ear (1954), Reik provides an elaboration and
extension of Freud's theory of the repetition:

> When we persuade the patient to proceed from action to remi-
> niscence, we are trying to lead him from an infantile method
> to one that came later in evolution and is more rational and
> comprehensible to us. (350)

Similar to Freud and his work on the role of repetition in the
natural world, Reik suggests a certain phylogenetic dimension to the
repetition. Here again we are placed at an exciting interface between
science and psychology. In drawing upon an evolutionary explanation

for replicative activity, we are looking at a set of universal, arche-typal habits that influence all of life. Here, the human, the fish, and the plant are subject to similar evolutionary trajectories in that each has to follow its own species-unique morphology.

Discussing the role of repetition in denying memory and affect, Reik cites a play by the Viennese writer J. N. Nestroy in which: " . . . a man is asked why he always carries a cane. He answers, 'I carry this cane in eternal memory of a girl whom I never want to think of again.'" (*Listening,* 349) While Reik, like Freud, stresses the defensive nature of the repetition, he also admits its vital importance to the psychic economy of the individual: "With a certain reservation we may say that the past cannot fade until it has again become present." (*Listening,* 348)

By considering the universality of the tendency to repeat found in the psyche and the natural world and that it is apparently necessary to the life process, the thinking of Reik and Freud becomes less reductive and more compelling. Consider Reik's fascinating observation that

> the validity of [the theory of repetition compulsion] extends far beyond individual life, and . . . the lasting, unconscious traces of ancestral experience are among the undiscover-able and yet effective factors determining our lives. (*Listening,* 352)

Reik's contribution to repetition theory leaves us again with an apparent paradox. As a psychological phenomenon within the human psyche, repetition often represents a primitive attempt at mastering painful, and at times terrifying, experiences. Yet the utilization of the repetition as a means of mastery is bound to fail. However, Reik is quick to point out the phylogenetic, evolutionary, and purposeful nature of the repetition compulsion. In this light, Reik, with Freud, helps to set the stage for a more exhaustive, compelling, and challenging investigation of this essential life instinct, leading to Jung's theory of the archetypes with which this chapter opened.

There is abundant, not to say serendipitous, evidence that the human imperative to repeat is a natural development and not merely a consciously derived construct. In the next chapter we will take a closer look at the meaning behind the drive to repeat, which springs from the inexhaustible source of the archetypes.

CHAPTER TWO

Patterns in Psyche and Nature

Virtually every facet of our lives is infused with the presence and subtle recognition of patterns. We wake up every morning and follow habitual patterns—making our first cup of coffee, preparing a bit of breakfast, reading the newspaper. Many of these morning activities occur virtually autonomously, as if they had a life of their own. Just think of the many commercials where some-one walks zombie-like into the kitchen for his morning coffee.

A strict behaviorist may explain these behaviors as learned and, like the powerful call for the first cup of coffee, as clearly indicative of our caffeine addiction. I must admit that I have been getting up between four and five a.m. to write this book, so I am thinking of my own morning coffee ritual. While a behaviorist or cognitive interpre-tation, which calls attention to the personal dimension of behavior and motivation, is logical, it is unable to address the broader meaning, implications, and goals of our collective tendency to create and respond to rituals.

The natural world is filled with patterns. Much of what we find remarkable and beautiful in the world has to do with our observation of them. Just a walk near the sea or in the mountains reminds us of their presence and power of attraction. Every child's first trip to the beach includes a hunt for seashells and playing with waves. Each seashell, while innately unique, grows in response to an inborn design—in accordance with its own archetypal and morphogenetic blueprint. Richard Ott, a surgeon and collector of rare seashells, pointed out to me in a private conversation that the underlying order, design, and growth of seashells corresponds to a universal order matching the Fibonnaci code. This mathematical code underscores the generation of many patterns found in the natural world and even in musical composition. In this area of morphogenetic studies, which has tremendous implications for our continuing investigations into the emergence of form from archetypal fields, the work of Mae-Wan Ho, Brian Goodwin, and Rupert Sheldrake has opened new areas of inquiry for the scientific and lay communities.

While patterns are ever present in the outer, natural world, we also see the clustering of archetypal material into recognizable patterns within the cultural and social domain. Each culture, in response to some intrinsic sense of meaning, creates rituals and customs expressive of it. For some, as in the Native Americans of the Pacific Northwest, we find the forest and the sea totemized. In the Arctic, the Inuit people look to the bear, the whale, and the snow as expressions of powerful forces of nature, which are understood to be manifestations of the divine and, in the classical Jungian sense, of the Self.

While archetypes are universal, each society is organized with its own specific alignments to them. Alignments, in this regard, are viewed as a type of tuning mechanism through which connections are made to specific facets of the archetype, but not to others. As we look at the artistic expressions of children from different groups, we can see how the various forms they create, as in their drawings of animals, etc., reflect externalizations of internal, dominant archetypal patterns. Perhaps the deep-seated need to represent images speaks to the compelling nature of patterns.

Roles such as teacher, hunter, farmer, healer, crafts person, child care worker, etc. exist in all cultures. The universality of these roles suggests the existence of some inborn, preexistent, archetypal, morphological blueprint that informs and guides the generation of form in these domains. Jung addressed this issue in the film, *Face to Face,* when he was asked about his belief in God. He explained that every culture since the beginning of time has included the notion of a deity.

14

He went on to say that this internal imperative suggests that the God concept is indeed archetypal—meaning universal and innate. Many of James Hillman's works, especially *The Soul's Code,* speak to the unfolding of internal morphology into form. For Jung, Hillman, Plato, and in my own ideas about the *a priori* nature of patterns, there appears to be agreement that matter emerges in response to and in accordance with a preformed image, or field. This image, or field, finds expression in matter with a specificity that matches the informational core of the archetype. The nature of the constellated archetype can be inferred from the form it assumes. Form emerges in response to a stable set of morphological processes and codes, which through successive generations have established a highly developed and recognizable pattern and design. The emergent properties of matter thus can be read as the materialization, incarnation, and reflection of psyche into matter.

Patterns exist as a clustering of preexistent information and energetic potential that then emerges into recognizable forms. This point may be more easily illustrated by describing the art and practice of mushroom hunting. Like my paternal grandfather from *Reggio Calabria* in Italy, I now take my son into the woods in search of edible mushrooms.

There are many levels of experience needed to collect edible mushrooms. The work involved is clearly worth the effort, as you will find if you have ever had a meal of wild mushrooms. One of the featured meals in Assisi, at our annual Assisi Conference entitled "The Confluence of Matter and Spirit," is *Pasta con Tartuffa,* an Umbrian dish made with wild truffles, which are still hunted by dogs as they were centuries ago.

When you first enter the woods to search for mushrooms, you may be lucky enough to find a mushroom here and there. However, eventually you begin to notice something fascinating—the clustering of mushrooms. Here we take a step deeper into the domain of patternicity and pattern recognition. Through the finding of one mushroom, we can predict that others exist nearby. So an important inference regarding a species and its habitat can be drawn through the observation of form found in a single mushroom. This holographic model of inferring the whole from the parts opens up new vistas in our understanding of the personal and collective psyche.

As we improve our observational skills, we realize the variety and diversity of mushrooms existing in the woods. While we may have initially only been familiar with the relatively tasteless button mushrooms we find in most American supermarkets, time in the woods provides access to an array of mushrooms in numerous colors, shapes, and sizes.

As we develop and cultivate a more detailed knowledge and appreciation of different types of mushrooms, we recognize that each will grow only in conditions suited to the unique needs of its species. We find that some grow better along the roadside and some by the water, while others will only grow on dying and decaying trees. Then the process becomes even more specific. We discover that a tree-growing variety will only grow on certain types of trees—like the oyster mushroom, which grows most often on decaying maple trees.

I find the specificity and the hand-and-glove fit between form and environment and between form and field fascinating for many reasons. Here we have entered the domain of archetypes and form, and in so doing we discover that emergent form is dependent upon specific, ambient conditions and factors. However we also realize that even before a form appears, it exists as a potential in the field. For instance, we can go to a site renowned for producing fine morel mushrooms and find nothing. Yet after two days of heavy rain, we may find a sudden emergence of these prized mushrooms. The same is true when we find a dying maple tree and know that within time we can expect to find oyster mushrooms. Here form is lying in potential, waiting for corresponding environmental conditions to arise so that the emergent properties of matter can be expressed. Ervin Laszlo made this point in saying: "Form exists as a potential in fields even before it appears in the outer world" (1993, Assisi Lecture).

While at first mushrooms seem to pop up randomly in the woods, we soon begin to understand the high degree of order existing both in their morphology and in their tendency to express. Through Laszlo's idea that field predates form, we can perhaps better understand Jung and Hillman's notions about the primacy of the image. The image, as a representative of a specific archetypal field, carries with it its own inherent morphology and information and, when accessed, entrains the individual or culture into that archetypal field.

At this stage in our mushroom foraging experiences, we have already accomplished the following:

-the capacity to see and find mushrooms in the woods

-an awareness of the diversity of color, shape, etc. among mushrooms

-an awareness of the clustering effect of mushrooms

-the knowledge of the specificity of form inherent in the emergent properties of mushrooms

-the intricate and highly detailed relationship existing between form and field and between form and environment.

The close fit between form and environment is captured in the following letter from *Nature* magazine. Commenting on a misplaced image in a cartoon, Wayne Van Vooffiles from the Department of Molecular and Cellular Biology at the University of Arizona writes:

> I have often enjoyed Birch's satirical cartoons on topical issues. He frequently includes clever symbols in his cartoons to emphasize his point. In the past few years, he has included drawings depicting events that have occurred in the Mojave Desert of California and in central New Mexico. Finding a Saguaro cactus in either of these locations would be a considerable range extension for this plant. The Saguaro cactus is endemic only to the North American Sonoran Desert. This limits its distribution in the United States to southern Arizona and extreme southeastern California. Saguaro cacti would not naturally be found in either of the locations where Birch has placed them. (*Nature*, March 21, 1996, 196)

17

The fact that nature has established such a close relationship between form and field speaks to a coherence between nature and organism. Perhaps this point will be more clearly illustrated through a discussion of the intricate and fascinating processes responsible for the generation of form in the human psyche and in the outer, natural world.

The Generation of Form

Patterns can be viewed as material representations of archetypal, informational fields expressed in space and time. They exist as external mappings of internal processes, be it morphogenetic promptings in the biological domain or symbolic, archetypal expressions found in the human psyche.

The emergence of form has fascinated mankind since the beginning of time. Jung's elucidation of alchemical texts reveals that their importance was in their understanding of the relationship between matter/form and psyche/spirit. In much the same vein as St. Francis, the alchemists viewed all expressions of matter in the outer world as physical representations of eternal, archetypal forms and processes.

As an organism begins the process of expressing its own innate, unique design, we see the unfolding of a series of intricate and fascinating dynamics. While each system, like each mushroom, responds to its own species-specific prompts, there exists a series of fundamental dynamics to which virtually every system responds in its quest for expression and development. The late Erich Janstch (1980), a highly regarded systems theorist, acknowledges these universal, archetypal dynamics when writing:

> Science is about to recognize these principles as general laws of the dynamics of nature. Applied to humans and their systems of life, they appear therefore as principles of a profoundly natural way of life. (*The Self Organizing Universe*, 8)

The processes responsible for the generation of form have been investigated in the human domain by child development specialists and psychologists, in the biological domain by structural biologists, and by systems theorists, chaos theorists, and theoretical physicists.

C. G. Jung's work on the nature of the archetype makes important contributions in this area. His idea about the *a priori* nature of the archetype is paralleled in David Bohm's work on "the Implicate Order" and, more recently, in Ervin Laszlo's work on "the *vacuum plenum*" field. All postulate that form and meaning emerge out of something—a generative potential that seems to be more encompassing and expansive than its temporal expression in emergent form. With the idea of form emerging out of a field, we see how Bohm's idea that the explicate order emerges from the implicate order relates to Laszlo's idea of form emerging out of a *vacuum plenum* field of pure potential and to Jung's idea that symbols and life emerge from an archetypal backdrop.

Central to the emergence of form in any system is the engagement in replicative, iterative processes. Replication involves the system's ability to engage in autopoetic processes through which its component parts work together to create a specific product or psychological regime. We can posit that replication is nature's way of conserving form and the innate properties of a system. Central also to the work of systems theorists and biologists is an understanding of how organisms and systems obtain the information needed for reproduction and how this information is converted into action and form.

To insure that each new form remains consistent with its ontological core, a system proceeds from potential to form by traversing its phylogenetic history. Phylogenetic replication of each new emergent form insures a resonance with past forms, thus creating a thriving and active bridge between the past and present. Janstch (1980) makes a similar point when suggesting that:

> The linking back to the origin not only restores strength, but also creates the possibility of recognizing and bringing into play ever new chreod[e]s and new developmental lines. (*The Self Organizing Universe,* 300)

Consider the fact that even before the act of conception, the overall form the fetus will eventually assume exists in a potential state of readiness. This potential is activated through a series of physical and psychological prompts that convert it into emergent form.

Survival and health in virtually every species is dependent on the successful translation and conversion of morphogenetic information into form and matter. Fidelity and exact duplication are crucial at this earliest developmental stage. Csanyi (1989) and Csanyi and Kampis (1985, 1991) have made important insights into the system's utilization of replicative processes.

Consider again the situation at conception. While each fetus is unique, near exact duplication means that there is little, if any, degree of freedom allowed while undergoing its earliest stage of emergence into life. As when a conductor provides the score for an orchestra and demands near perfect imitation of the composer's vision of the piece, so too nature, genetics, and psyche demand near perfect duplication of a biological, and perhaps even an archetypal, code. Clearly, creativity, uniqueness, and diversity are essential in the development of life, but not so much at the beginning stage of life. Jantsch (1980) makes this point when writing: "starting conditions [for the creation of life] . . . are perhaps relatively narrowly limited" (*The Self Organizing Universe*, 9).

Patterning and Form

Through the engagement of replicative phenomena, systems and organisms assume a design unique to their species and field. This design, which is strengthened by the system's historical past, represents a high degree of fidelity to prior form and the specific evolutionary trajectory unique to that system. A form and shape of the organism emerges that is consistent with others of its species. In this regard, I am defining a pattern as a coalescing of multiple trajectories into a singularity. As prior form establishes a history and becomes patterned through its repeated iterations, we can again speak of a clearly defined morphology. However, it appears that morphology, like the archetype, is preexistent. For instance, we can identify a rose with relative ease and differentiate it from a cactus because every rose has a characteristic design with specific features. This design, which I will call archetypal, is the physical representation of an archetype. The archetype assumes a form whose features match the informational constant of that archetype. Here we begin to appreciate matter as a specific physical incarnation of the archetype.

This appreciation of matter follows in the tradition of the alchemists, who also emphasize the presence of spirit in matter, and of Goodwin, who attempts to collapse the duality between organism and field. Clearly, this idea has many implications for the sciences, psychology, and our general understanding of human nature. While these points will be elaborated a bit later in this book, I will say that an important inference that can be made involves an appreciation of matter, not as an isolated or frozen event in space and time, but as the psyche's attempt to present in symbolic form the face of an archetype. From the recognition of an archetypal morphology, we can then look at form—be it a rose, a cactus, or, in the human domain, as the partner we choose or the theory to which we subscribe—as an expression of an archetype which draws and entrains us into alignment with it.

The archetype, which functions as an informational, rational, and meaning-carrying structure, creates a field of influence whose effect is not limited by space and time parameters and often consumes individual consciousness as it works to incarnate through the situations, obsessions, interests, concerns, relationships, and moods we experience. The presence of the archetype is felt through its effects. Here one may wonder why I invoke the concept of a field—used in the natural world to describe gravitational or electromagnetic fields, for example,—to explain archetypal influences. The reason is that in no other domain in the natural world do we see the rearrangement of matter occurring in response to some seemingly hidden influence. Consider the ability of a magnet to rearrange previously disparate pieces of iron filings into a design, or the gravitational force, which keeps our feet planted on the ground. Currently, research is under way

21

to examine the effect of specific electromagnetic fields on individuals and our physiology. For example, Robert Becker (1990) identifies the damaging, and even carcinogenic, effects of living near high-energy transmission wires and, to a lesser degree, of being exposed repeatedly to fluorescent lighting. These examples speak to the power of a field to restructure matter into alignments consistent with its particular properties.

An interesting example occurred when my son, Chris, and I were out fishing one day, and I was fortunate enough to hook a large mouth bass. Wanting my son to share in the excitement of the catch (just for the record, we eat virtually everything we catch or throw back fish that are too small), I handed him the fishing rod and asked him to help. He took the rod and brought the fish close enough to the boat for us to see how large it was. Suddenly though, it made a run toward the back of the boat, ripped the line on the propeller, and swam away. I suggested to Chris that we look at our books on fish when we got home. Our books provide an exciting way to learn about patterns and fields because they describe the habitat, feeding habits, and other characteristics of each particular fish. What a great find for us to read that one should consider himself lucky to hook a large mouth bass. However, the author advised that, when fishing for large mouth bass, one should take his outboard motor out of the water, since this type of fish will usually head for the back of the boat, wrap the line around the engine, and break free. In our shared amazement over how this description so accurately mirrored our experience, my son asked if the fish had read the same book. The fish's behavior was obviously consistent with the highly specific properties of its field.

These examples speak to the power of a field to restructure matter into alignment with its particular properties. From these and similar observations, I have developed the following definition of field:

> A field is the energetic component of an archetype, which exerts its influence over space and time. This influence is not bound by space and time constraints. Rather, we find that in contrast to fields in the outer

22

world which are space-time dependent, such as gravitational and electromagnetic fields, archetypal fields are
nonlocal, as evidenced, for instance, in telepathy,
synchronicities, and the non-local transmission of
information, etc. Essential to the concept of archetypal
fields is the finding that they are dynamic, not static,
and involve interrelationships.

While physical fields, such as gravitational fields, are highly
dependent on space-time parameters—gravitational force, for example,
is reduced at a distance—an archetypal field exerts its influence as if
its force is carried through a "frictionless, fluid medium." We can
glimpse its influence at a distance and its tendency to work across
space-time parameters.

F. David Peat adds an important perspective when stating that:

The fact that a force is reduced by distance is not to do
with the friction but the volume in which the force
applied increases. By analogy, the amount of water fall-
ing on a square foot of ground from a circular spray falls
off with distance. But if you use a focused stream, from
a hose pipe, this need not be true. What you need is an
influence that does not depend upon the amplitude of a
force but on its form. (i.e. something like Bohm's active
information). In this case the influence does not fall off
with distance. Or you need some sort of non-local influence. But a force carried through a frictionless, fluid
medium (which sounds like the old idea of ether) is still
going to fall off with distance. (personal communication)

The archetypal field is thus different from other fields in its nonlocality.
In this regard, we see the relationship between Bohm's theory of the
"Implicate Order," which expresses itself through the explicate order,
and my own view of archetypal fields.

To illustrate the overwhelming power of the archetype to con-
sume and absorb individual and collective consciousness, consider
the atrocities in Nazi Germany, which occurred under the sway of the

Wotan archetype. This archetype, which found a physical and human manifestation in the personage of Adoph Hitler, took over an entire country, in fact, the entire world, compelling individuals to engage in activities otherwise unthinkable.

The archetype's power to entrain and draw individuals and entire nations into its orbit suggests the need to reassert and reinvestigate Jung's findings regarding the strength and autonomy of the psyche. In much the same manner as an attractor site—be it magnetic or archetypal—serves to draw the trajectory of a system into a specific region (or, as it is termed in chaos theory, a basin of attraction), so too does the archetype work through the creation of an attractor. The attractor is the complex. The complex, as defined by Jungian Analyst Yoram Kaufmann, is a quanta of energy organized around a certain theme— for instance, a mother complex, a father complex, a sexual complex, etc. The complex, like the attractor, functions as a magnetic epicenter creating the convergence of archetypal potentialities into a singularity, a highly patterned behavioral tendency, drawing to it one specific facet of an archetype. For instance, there is a great deal of variation in the mother complex so that it is a bit vague to say simply that someone has a mother complex. Rather, we need to identify with which particular facet of the mother archetype the individual is aligned.

The complex, in this case the mother complex, attracts and creates resonance patterns with like experiences, which become an expression of an archetypal component. F. David Peat's book (1987), *Synchronicity: The Bridge Between Mind and Matter,* is filled with examples of this phenomenon. The complex creates a type of antenna around us so that we can tune into and align with a specific frequency of an archetype. This tuning mechanism determines which frequency will be accessed and which will be tuned out. For instance, I suspect that many of us have gone through times when we were dealing with an issue that suddenly manifested in virtually every facet of our lives. This tuning process is a complicated, fascinating, and surprisingly exacting phenomenon. It works by creating alignments and entrainments with only those segments of life that match the archetypal constants of the constellated archetype.

A reductionist may suggest that this specialized tuning can be simply explained as a conscious selection process through which the individual may choose by what he will or will not be influenced. However, when we realize the consistency of archetypal expression and see the high degree of synchronistic experiences constellated around it, we are forced to consider that this process involves much more than personal selection. Cognitive or behavioral theory is limited in its understanding of phenomena because it seeks explanations solely in the domain of the personal experiences, desires, and history of the individual.

Subjective theory is effective in uncovering the subjective dynamics of experience, but its focus on the personal overlooks those nonpersonal, transpersonal, archetypal factors that orient and guide much of life. Instead, we do well to realize the autonomy of these archetypal dynamics and see that individual consciousness has little to do with the actual activation of the alignment. Here we can consider the unfolding of the archetype as the manifestation of a fated factor intrinsic to the individual's life. I bring in the element of fatedness since the overarching archetypal field tends to create an enduring influence similar to the influence of one's birth order or cultural and spiritual inheritance. Like them, the field is a carrier of the destiny factor and provides an orientational blueprint for life.

Consciousness, however, becomes a central player when it comes to metabolizing the content and imperative of the complex. At this time, we need to step out of the spin and possessive hold of the complex to make conscious meaning of the process. As the complex tunes into a specific facet of the archetype and draws to it like experiences, we find that matter assumes the face of an archetypal alignment in a recognizable form. It is recognizable in the sense that the archetype is a universal constant. While there is a great deal of divergence in the way parenting, for instance, is practiced in the human and animal kingdom, the experience of parenting is still a constant. In many societies, we find the traditional parenting model lived out with two individuals assuming specific roles. However, great variation exists as to who assumes what role. In Amazonian cultures, for example, men often raise the children while the women hunt. In the animal world, we also find variations upon this archetypal theme. Some male birds are the food gatherers for the nesting females. The male sea horse, as another example, gestates the young in its own body. What *is* constant is the experience and need for parenting. While this archetype is expressed in various ways, its core meaning—its ontology—and mandate remain constant. The primary task of parenting is to care for what is young, needy, virtually helpless, and highly dependent on its caretakers. Parenting is not solely expressed by becoming a parent to a child but can be experienced whenever something is new and needs a great deal of attention.

Perhaps we can better understand the idea of archetypal constants through an illustration. Imagine that extraterrestrials come to earth hoping to understand our customs. As they observe us, they will see the universal need of humans to find shelter. Be it a straw hut, the cardboard box of a bagperson, a tent, a one-story home, or a palatial estate, we are all driven by some *a priori* need to create a home. Even if these aliens know absolutely nothing about our world, they will nevertheless notice how each of us spends a considerable amount of time and resources in the pursuit of a home. And, while there will always be many personal and cultural variations, the archetypal core of the search for shelter remains a constant. Through the act of finding a home, we fulfill an important archetypal need that has as its goal the creation of a structure within which to live one's life. This is the ontology of the archetype.

I would like to add just a word here about problematic, non-generative alliances with archetypal mandates. When parents abandon their young or exhibit severe character disturbances resulting in their inability to properly care for their children, we then have a stable alignment to the archetype of the abandoning parent. While I initially viewed these alignments as faulty, as misalignments, I now realize that each particular expression of parenting is consistent with a highly specific archetypal alignment. So, while the alignment may be non-generative, as in cases where parents abandon their children, it nonetheless remains archetypal in nature, even though abusive and destructive.

To illustrate, I was recently involved in a case where an intelligent, divorced woman refused to financially contribute either to her child's education or therapy. While the father accepted full responsibility for both, in addition to paying a substantial amount in monthly child support and maintaining fifty percent of the physical custody, the mother, who was in good health, chose to only work part time. This woman unfortunately had a non-generative alignment with the bountiful mother archetype. If it had been a case of financial or medical hardship, her reluctance to pay would have been understandable. However, the mandate of parenting is focused upon caring for the young and often results in a certain amount of hardship and sacrifice for parents, many of whom take on extra work to ensure the best possible education for their children. Given this mandate, we find a serious flaw in the mother's pattern of behavior.

We could easily interpret this pattern as one in which the mother maintains a less than helpful attitude toward the child. Additionally, we could anticipate the continuance of the pattern and make a highly probable prediction about this woman's mothering tendencies. While we should always hope for change from non-generative alignments, it is prudent to be realistic in assessing the degree of dissonance between the archetypal mandate and the expression of that archetype in the individual. In doing so, we can then see the costs involved in subsidizing such a change.

The attracting quality of the archetype seeks commonality of experience and a universally recognizable expression of form. Here we enter the domain of the archetypal core of the pattern. Archetypes are *a priori* and find expression in relatively stable ways. Erich Neumann (1954) suggests that specific images cluster around specific archetypes. He terms such a grouping of symbols a symbol canon. As groupings of symbols become synonymous with par-

27

ticular archetypal constellations, they coalesce into discernible and recognizable patterns.

Jung is quick to point out the distinction between his view of the symbol and Freud's. What Freud mistakenly terms a symbol is really a sign. A sign—like a stop sign—has a known content. Jung, on the other hand, looked to the meaning and teleological dimension of the symbol, focusing on its attempt to express some particular quality of the archetype and on its role in carrying new information and experiences to the individual. Additionally, the symbol stands as an orientational marker serving to draw the individual into alignment with a particular archetypal field. (The term "orientational marker" comes from Dr. Yoram Kaufmann's work and is discussed in his article, "The Way of the Image.") So while on first glance one may view the image of a child at the mother's breast as an expression of the child's personal wish or experience of its mother, Jung understood the image in its larger, archetypal context as having to do with nurturing. The image points to an alignment, either generative or regressive, needing attention in the individual's life.

Similarly, Neumann (1954) emphasizes the archetypal backdrop of symbolism and human experience. To illustrate, he points to the image and experience of the womb as essentially archetypal, explaining that while everyone has a personal experience of the womb, its ontology is a universal (archetypal) constant, stretching far beyond personal experience. The archetypal womb—a container which is individually experienced—exists as the womb of humanity out of which all of life and creativity emerge. Archetypal material thus finds symbolic expression in recognizable forms that, through constant reiterations throughout time, become relatively stable configurations coalescing into familiar patterns.

Pattern recognition is essential for the preservation of life. Animals quickly learn to observe patterns. The sudden silence in a previously noisy desert may signal danger to certain vulnerable species. The gradual drop in temperature and the appearance of acorns are a familiar and recognizable pattern alerting a squirrel to the onset of winter. The inability to read patterns—like those that indicate the beginning of winter, for example—will be disastrous for the squirrel. Every individual is born with and continues developing these highly tuned perceptual skills that help to read patterns in the outer, and hopefully in the inner, world. We quickly sense who can be trusted and who to avoid. Similarly our taste buds quickly learn to differentiate between healthy and spoiled food. Even the autoimmunological system can be viewed as a highly tuned pattern-recognition system that constantly monitors the cellular and viral patterns of antigens in the body.

The medical field is yet another area where we see the tremendous value of pattern recognition. A respected colleague and friend, the late Dr. Robert Hook, explained that much of his medical training involved pattern recognition. On medical rounds the teaching physician would ask the interns to observe symptoms and see if they coalesced into a recognizable pattern. For example, a swelling of the glands, when coupled with a high temperature and other symptoms, indicates a particular syndrome or illness, and the recognition of this pattern of symptoms makes the illness more easily identifiable. The same is true for the coupling and grouping together of archetypal symbols, as we will see in the following section.

Patterns in Literature, Fairy Tales, and Life

The appearance and development of patterns are found throughout the world of literature. Virtually every story revolves around a character and plot, which as the story develops, coalesces into a familiar and recognizable pattern. For instance, my son enjoys watching "Scooby Doo," a cartoon about a group of teenagers and their faint of heart, yet heroic, dog Scooby Doo. After watching the first few minutes of an episode, you can easily anticipate the story's outcome. While most literature is not nearly as predicable, it frequently follows an *a priori,* archetypal developmental pattern. In order to fulfill a certain literary theme and goal, a number of highly specific scenes, incidents, and characterizations must be developed. The staging of the drama is carried out for the purpose of enhancing and explicating the theme. We can see how many dramas follow seemingly archetypal roads in search of their destinations. This suggests a relationship between archetype, pattern, and destiny.

Rollo May (1981) writes:

> The verb form of the word, destine, is defined as "to ordain, to devote, to consecrate." Destiny is a cognate of the term destination, which implies moving towards a goal. (*Freedom and Destiny,* 93)

Describing the relationship between an individual and fate, May writes that: "Hubris is the refusal to accept one's destiny" (100). The film *Forest Gump* illustrates the sense of being gripped by fate. Lieutenant Dan, whose lineage includes many war heroes dating back to the Civil War who gave up their lives for their country, is caught in blind obedience to fate. At one point, Forest Gump carries the severely wounded Dan to safety. Dan yells at Gump and demands to be left alone because he believes that he must die in combat. In being saved, Dan feels cheated out of the role of the tragic war hero. Here we find a seemingly fated goal to which Dan is inextricably linked. Forest Gump's intervention, however, offers the possibility of breaking Dan of his archetypal possession.

Dan needed to develop a personal relationship to his fate. In the following, Rollo May helps us to understand the work involved in transforming fate into destiny:

> The radical shift from determinism to destiny occurs when the subject is self-conscious about what is happening to him or her. The presence of consciousness creates the context in which the human being's responses to his or her destiny occur. (88)

Many of our greatest films, such as *Gone with the Wind* and Lina Wertmuller's recent, although lesser known, *Ciao Professore,* proceed through a series of twists and turns before arriving at their final lysis and conclusion. While I do not mean to suggest that they possess a "canned" or static quality, these films nonetheless reflect a strong connection to archetypal patterns. Part of what makes them so compelling is their capacity to represent archetypal situations that, through their universality, inevitably touch us all. Consider the enduring quality of Frank Capra's *It's a Wonderful Life* or the play *Fiddler on the Roof.* In *Fiddler,* we are drawn into the joys and the heartbreaking ordeals of the characters, who are faced with threats to both their homes and their treasured traditions. Who cannot shed a tear when listening to parents sending off their child into marriage, so beautifully captured in the song "Sunrise, Sunset." Or not mourn with Tony and Maria as they sing in *West Side Story* "There's a Place for Us." These archetypal events involve situations that humanity has encountered since the beginning of time. Life, love, death, the struggle of opposites, good and evil, mortality—these are all nodal points in the human experience. Archetypal situations thus exist as *a priori* potentialities in the psyche and are expressed through dreams, fantasies, and couplings, as well as in literature, films, and plays, carrying with them highly patterned modes of experience.

Another important carrier of archetypal information is the fairy tale. Through tales of kings and queens, heroes and dragons, and the many variations of mother-son/daughter and father-daughter/son relationships, fairy tales bring us back to a world where archetypal functioning proceeds without the filtering influence of consciousness. These tales, which span many generations and are told in many different countries, represent the unique perspective of the archetypes. Jung made a similar point when stating:

> These fantasy-images undoubtedly have their closest analogues in mythological types. We must therefore assume that they correspond to certain *collective* (and not personal) structural elements of the human psyche in general, and, like the morphological elements of the human body, are *inherited. (CW 9i,* § 262)

As these stories are told and retold, they assume a numinous force, not only because of their repeated inclusion in the culture, but

31

because of their persistence in presenting a particular point of view.

With a bit of training, we can learn to identify the underlying archetypal themes in fairy tales. The late Marie-Louise von Franz was perhaps the world's foremost interpreter of fairy tales. In her book, *Archetypal Patterns in Fairy Tales,* she shares her observations of more than forty years in investigating their archetypal underpinnings:

> You could call the archetype the "nature constant" of the human psyche. It is eminently conservative, and furthermore it always eliminates impurities that have been added by individual problems. On account of that, we have in the classical folk tales an end product which represents in the form of symbolic images certain typical collective unconscious processes. Since fairy tales have a form by which they naturally repeat themselves, they are one of the best kinds of source material for studying the "nature constants" of the collective psyche .... In fairy tales, too we find all the elements of the process of individuation, or sequences that are clearly parallel to what we can observe in the process of individuation. (*Archetypal Patterns in Fairy Tales,* 17)

The archetype finds a relatively stable mode of representation through symbols expressing its core pattern. As a result of the relative stability of form and theme in the expression of archetypal patterns, we can often infer the nature of the constellated archetype through its representation in the story. Each fairy tale is composed of numerous images organized around a central theme. We can observe a high degree of thematic congruity running throughout each story. So while the different characters and actions may at first appear to be a collection of randomly selected and disparate elements, we soon begin to see how each image is intricately connected to the other and, as an aggregate, coalesces into a finely tuned, patterned mosaic. Here the story expresses its particular theme by drawing to it characters, incidents, and settings unique to the specific morphology of the archetype. For instance, the archetype of the dying king will inevitably involve a tale about a once powerful leader who unwittingly meets his end through the appearance of a new ruler. While at first glance the relationship between character, plot, and archetype may seem apparent, what is less obvious is the intricate web connecting the images to one another. Through the entrainment and alignment of images to a central, overarching theme, we come to learn the nature of the constellated archetype.

Consider the Sicilian fairy tale (Calvino, *Italian Fairytales,* 666-668) "The Boy Who Fed the Crucifix" as an illustration of these ideas. The story opens with a farmer driving down the road and finding a young, abandoned boy. The fact that the story begins by highlighting the older male/young boy relationship suggests a father-son theme. And, through its omission, we can also infer that the story concerns the effects of the missing mother and the feminine in the lives of the father and son.

While the above observations are relatively simple, the inferences we can draw about the developmental concerns embedded in the story and the personal and archetypal initiatory rites of passage required for someone in this specific situation are quite rich. There is an extensive mythology and history of boys raised by their fathers alone and the effect of the missing mother. We know that such a boy will have to learn certain characteristically male behavioral and archetypal patterns. Also, we know that the effect of the missing mother will in all likelihood create challenges to the boy's capacity to relate to the world of matter-mother and to internal psychic reality in general.

A similar process of archetypal pattern recognition is found in dreams, where the archetype also expresses itself in universally familiar ways. If, for instance, the dream begins with "I am going to my mother's house . . . , " we can infer that the dreamer is involved in the process of learning to negotiate the archetypal world of mothers. Mothers here are not meant strictly in the personal sense but rather in the collective, archetypal sense. The archetypal mother relates to one's internal life and often to the ability to express internal reality and potentiality in the outer world. So, while the specific details of an individual's life cannot necessarily be understood through a particular clustering of images, they do provide us with access to a great deal of information. Here the clustering of images serves as an orientational marker.

In much the same manner as a map indicates to what town each road leads, the image indicates which aspect of the archetype is activated. So the father/son fairy tale is about the psychic situation in the father/son relationship, and the dream of the mother's house is about the individual's relationship to the world of mothers. More specific information is revealed when we discover more details about the image. For instance, when we learn about the specific qualities and characteristics of the father or mother in the fairy tale or dream, we can determine to what facet of the father and mother archetype the person is aligned.

Furthering this metaphor, the map to a town simply provides directions to it. However, more specific information about the town can be learned by visiting it, speaking with the townfolk, and learning about its history. Through these activities one can discover its unique nature and hopefully in time identify its specific ontology. Similarly, think of traveling across Europe and the many different cultures, languages, foods, and traditions that are unique to each country and region. For instance, my annual trip to Italy provides access to the Italian psyche, the home of my ancestors. Just walk down the streets of Assisi, the famed town of St. Francis, and take in the aromas of the sauces cooking for the midday and evening meals. Listen to the church bells and catch a glimpse of the local people to see into the Italian soul. Italians insist on having the best education for their children, the highest quality food for their table, clothes, wine, art, and generally are willing to make substantial sacrifices to maintain these values.

The details of each culture's traditions and daily rituals further clarify its archetypal nature. For instance, the town of Assisi and its environs are uniquely wedded to St. Francis's relationship to matter and psyche. There is something about the site of Assisi that draws people into the field of matter-spirit concerns—those same issues St.

Francis struggled with throughout his life. Here we can posit that a relationship exists between site and archetype, which in many respects is the purview of the field of geomorphology and may offer a plausible explanation for the "power sites" located around the world. Assisi, Italy is certainly one such site.

We can fine-tune our capacity to recognize patterns by staying with the illustration of Italian culture and considering the regional differences found in various parts of Italy. For instance, Milan in the north, and Naples and Sicily in the south reflect differences in the respective psyches of their citizens. Each archetypal field carries with it a series of mandates, tendencies, behaviors, and influences, and individuals within these fields will inevitably be affected by them. As in every archetypal field, a trip to Sicily brings with it its own set of specific archetypal experiences, which entrains and influences everyone drawn there.

As an island, Sicily is embedded in the mythology and psyche of islands and island people that have as main features isolation, solidarity, and separation. Here we begin to see the relationship between archetypes and geomorphology in that place carries with it highly charged properties. The history of Sicily reveals a troubled past. Because of its strategic location and the riches of its land, it was both coveted and conquered by many different peoples. Still today we find remnants of Norman and Arabic influences in Sicily's food, language, and architecture. The Sicilian dialect, which is what my family speaks, pronounces the letter "P" with a "B" sound. So *pizza*, becomes *u-bizza*, and *cipola* (onion) becomes *cibudda*. Further, the letter "O" is written and pronounced as a "U;" *formaggio* becomes *fumaggio*. Consider also the openness of the Neapolitans' usage of "A" instead of "U" as the article preceding words. We find Neopolitans saying *a bizza* and Tuscans *la pizza*, compared to the Sicilian *u bizza*. One senses a strong guttural resonance in these words, in addition to a certain vocal restriction in the Sicilian pronunciation, which I interpret as suggesting a constrained and troubled history.

35

Also dominant and archetypal in the Sicilian psyche is a deep sense of distrust for outsiders and a strong need to create and protect boundaries. During the late Middle Ages, when the French threatened to take over the island, Sicilians designed an ingenious method for identifying these intruders. They knew the French had difficulty pronouncing the word *ceci,* which is a type of bean. So a Sicilian would walk up to a stranger appearing in his village, start talking about food, and inevitably bring up the subject of *ceci* beans. As the Frenchman struggled with its pronunciation, the Sicilian quickly recognized him as an enemy and would do whatever was necessary to protect his family and home.

By the time I entered analysis at the age of twenty-four, I was steeped in the ambiance of the Sicilian temperament. While growing up in the streets of Brooklyn, our family's personal and archetypal roots were still closely connected to Sicily. In analysis, I would describe my life, attitudes, and the general way I went about life to my white Anglo-Saxon analyst. Hearing these stories, he would often just stare out the window and tell me how paranoid I was. Like my ancestors before me, I too quickly realized the presence of danger and that my analyst would never understand the Sicilian way. I told him that I was not paranoid, but was instead Sicilian. Failing to understand the Sicilian and southern Italian psyche and its translation and continued influence in second and third generation Italians in Brooklyn, he simply framed my behavior according to his own upbringing and biases. He neglected to see what was archetypally inherited in my behaviors and attitudes. Without this cultural awareness, he viewed my behaviors as inappropriate. However, when viewed from their archetypal perspective, they can be better understood. Just as we have a genetic inheritance, we also have an archetypal, cultural legacy. Each carries its own significance and history and demands to be understood from its own perspective.

With this foray into the Italian and Sicilian psyche, we see how language, behaviors, rituals, and tendencies exist as archetypal constants in the psyche and reveal the underlying archetypal morphology of the individual and culture. While each archetypal morphology is

36

unique, its expression within a particular culture creates characteristic patterns. These patterns become pervasive within the culture, and their archetypal roots are evidenced in its members.

Residents as well as visitors are influenced by a country's prevailing spirit and national identity. While in the medieval city of Assisi, the more than one million visitors a year who are drawn to visit it experience the power of the Umbrian hills and often come to understand why St. Francis loved this town. Similar to what New England's Native Americans speak of as places of power (*manitou*), there are sites located around the world that for centuries have been revered as sacred and filled with their own *mana*. Assisi is such a place. Scientific studies conducted at many of these sites reveal the presence of higher than normal electromagnetic frequencies. If these findings are correct, they may provide a scientific explanation for why people are affected by place and how places express certain archetypal constants.

Similarly, Robert Becker's studies (1990) explain how electromagnetic fields are responsible for many fascinating and alarming occurrences. Explaining their generative and life-enhancing effects, Becker discusses regenerative activity in salamanders. While the presence of regenerative activity has been well known and documented for years, the actual mechanics of how a limb can be regenerated from seemingly nothing has remained a mystery. Becker describes experiments where, following the amputation of a salamander's limb, a specific electromagnetic frequency signal localized at the wound site suddenly appears. The activation of these electromagnetic frequencies stimulates regenerative activity in the salamander as well as in other species, including the newt and starfish. Closely monitoring the events surrounding the sudden appearance of these fields, Becker found that another fascinating event occurred. Typically:

> The most familiar growth process is the healing of minor wounds. If the cut on your finger is deep enough, you know that you'll be left with a scar after it heals. This results from the most common form of healing ... known as fibrosis. Fibrosis is a relatively simple clos-

> ing of the wound edges with a fibrous tissue called col-
> lagen, made by specialized fibroblast cells. (*Cross
> Currents,* 28)

However, the salamander's regenerative activity is far from typical and involves a different process. Becker found that the cells, rather
than forming a fibrosis, underwent what he called dedifferentiation. Essential to the regenerative formation of new limbs is the
process where:

> a mass of primitive cells appears between the cut end of
> the stump ... This mass of embryonic cells is called the
> blastema, and is the raw material from which the new
> limb *will* grow . . . This process of "re-winding the tape"
> of embryonic growth is called dedifferentiation, and is
> the key element in bringing about regeneration. (*Cross
> Currents,* 34)

Becker further describes dedifferentiation as:

> ... the process in which a mature, specialized cell returns
> to its original, embryonic, unspecialized state. During dedi-
> fferentiation the genes that code for all other cell types are
> made available for use by depressing them. (305)

The dynamics of dedifferentiation and its role in creating new
life further validate my own findings about replicative dynamics in
the human psyche. It seems to me that prior to the emergence of new
life and form, there is inevitably a return to the earliest developmental
levels. This appears to happen when archetypal, morphological constants are reactivated.

Becker has also described the use of electromagnetism in medical practice, noting that electromagnetism has been used since the
1940s to increase bone density in humans. Regarding its more detri-
mental effects, he reports frequent migraines among computer operators
and a high incidence of cancer in the progeny of workers at high-
energy transmission stations. The connection between Becker's work

on electromagnetic fields and cultural and archetypal fields is that each involves the overriding presence of unseen forces that dramatically affect the arrangement and rearrangement of matter. While we cannot see these fields directly, their presence can be inferred by their affect on matter.

A further illustration of the existence of archetypal fields comes from a childhood experience that I still recall. When I was five years old, we visited my mother's uncle Tommy, whom I had never met. He had been quite sick. Unaware of the severity of his illness, we found him in great pain. My mother was visibly shaken, as were others in the room. While I was clearly affected by the personal feelings and emotions of family members, I also recall feeling the presence of something else in the room—something I had never experienced before. There was a slight, stale sick-room odor in the air, but yet the presence I sensed was more than the smells and more than the sight of my uncle in his sick bed. This sense of presence was more than my family's emotions too, yet somehow the combination of the emotions, the smells, and this other, underlying autonomous presence, created a haunting sense I can still feel. Now forty-three years after that event, I can see that what I felt as a young child was the chilling presence of a death field. When I discussed this memory with my mother, she reminded me that I had in fact definitively stated that death was in the room.

One may suggest that it was the strength of my family members' emotions that created my sensation of a death field and that I was simply experiencing my family's collective grief. I really do not believe that such stirring events are understandable through causal-reductive explanations. On the contrary, I believe that, as my uncle approached the transition from life to death, he was already embedded in a death field. It was the archetype of death, which everyone will at some point experience, that created the impressions and experiences shared by everyone in attendance. While the archetype of death and the field created around it exist independently of space-time parameters, its effects often occur locally.

FIELD, FORM, AND FATE

I revisited the death field just three years ago when my mother passed away after a long illness. The same feelings, sensations, and even smells permeated our home. She provided further evidence of the existence of this field when, in a semi-comatose state, she called out for her mother and, interestingly enough, for her long-deceased cousin Frankie, whom she had not spoken of for almost ten years. Crying out repeatedly from a morphine-induced unconsciousness, she said: "I want to go home. Can I please go home now? I want to be with my mother. Please, let me go home." These pleadings continued until she died early one morning.

Can we really reduce these emotions and experiences to a bio-chemical reaction or to purely personal factors? Can any reductive, causal, mechanistic explanation account for the high degree of similarity and regularity found in the way people approach death and handle the loss of a loved one? While not dismissing the influence and role of biochemical processes in stimulating certain near death experiences, I sense we do well to look beyond spatio-temporal factors and into the influence of non-local archetypal fields for greater insight into these mysterious processes.

Fields of Influence: An Archetypal Field Theory

Jung's theory of the archetypes, along with investigations in modern science, discusses the presence and power of field-generated phenomena. I realize the difficulties inherent in using the word "field" to describe the influencing effect of archetypes. Fields are used in mathematics and science to refer to operations occurring within a three-dimensional plane. They are space-time dependent processes, and their effects—like those, for instance, of the gravitational field—can be measured and predicted. Archetypal fields, on the other hand, appear to function non-locally. Their influence is not space-time dependent; and, from what we can tell, they are not subject to causal limitations as are fields in the outer, natural world.

PATTERNS IN PSYCHE AND NATURE

The presence of fields can be inferred from their effects. Electromagnetic and gravitational fields, for example, dramatically affect matter, rearranging and reconfiguring it. Archetypal fields also have this ability. I began publishing my ideas in this area in 1987. I speculated that archetypal fields contain specific energetic charges. However, one must distinguish between the commonly accepted scientific understanding of energy and the notion of an archetype having an energetic charge. The sense that archetypes contain energy that produces palpable emotions is really not so difficult to grasp. Situations such as the above-mentioned experience of death, along with the birth and death of a child or the emotional tone felt around a dinner table, all suggest that our individual and collective emotions are generated by the archetypes of life, death, etc. Each of these situations creates an ambiance that produces an emotional response.

As evidenced in the formation and organization of cultures, nations, families, and the individual psyche, each is guided by the presence of a force moving forward on many occasions toward a particular goal. Jung and his colleagues, Esther Harding and Marie-Louise von Franz, often spoke of psychic energy as the force driving the unfolding of events. However physical energy assumes a different form than psychic or archetypal energy in that the latter may not be measurable by standards and instruments currently available. Jung often said that the psyche resists being fit into customary definitions and works in a mercurial way to evade reductionistic interpretation. However, when we see the specific effects archetypes exert on individuals experiencing similar events, such as marriage, parenthood, or even death, there is a commonality of experience that dissolves individual distinctions. Clearly, individual variations exist, but they emerge out of a highly patterned, archetypal backdrop.

For this and other reasons, I sense that archetypal energetic charges may contain some force or influencing ability, albeit nonlocal and not of a physical, energetic form. Perhaps it would be more accurate to speak of these archetypal dynamics in terms of influences rather than forces. In a recent conversation, F. David

Peat mentioned that he was:

> even wondering if "energy" can only be defined in a
> local way and that the concept of "energy" does not
> exist in a non-local domain. Or maybe it's trans-
> formed into something else when it becomes
> non-local. (private conversation)

The use of fields to describe archetypes and their effects seems appropriate, since we now have a wealth of information about the archetype's ability to effect, transform, and possess individuals and cultures. Each field and each archetypal alignment—like the daughter/missing father field—carries its own specific, energetic signature, which is unique and consistent with the underlying morphology of the activated archetype. However, as Ervin Laszlo (1996) and Victor Mansfield (1995), an astrophysicist at Colgate University, pointed out in a discussion, both gravity and electromagnetic forces are space dependent. The force of electromagnetic and gravitational fields is reduced at a distance; it functions in proportion to the distance between the object and the field. Yet as Jung and his colleague and friend physicist Wolfgang Pauli pointed out, the archetype is an a-causal phenomenon, and its effects are not space-time dependent or governed by the laws of causality. This suggests that archetypal fields cannot be gauged and measured by currently known laws of physics. F. David Peat, who has already made substantial contributions to our understanding of matter, psyche, and energy, adds:

> I don't see an exact parallel between archetypal fields and
> electromagnetic [ones]. The latter are local, carry energy, and
> operate with mechanical forces. I think the former are fields
> of "form," non-local and may only carry what could perhaps
> be called "subtle energy." On the other hand we are also both
> [referring to the work of Conforti and Peat] leaning towards a
> second sort of energy-carrying field that is localized around
> two people or a landscape. (personal communication)

42

PATTERNS IN PSYCHE AND NATURE

Both Bell's theorem and the Einstein-Podolsky-Rosen (EPR) experiments found a mysterious degree of correlation and symmetry occurring between objects separated in space and time. Somehow, within the quantum world, objects seemed to influence one another despite being separated from one another. This anomaly defied all known laws of classical and modern physics. Similarly, while archetypal phenomena occur and are manifested within the space-time coordinates of everyday life, their matrix resides in some realm beyond, perhaps in the "Implicate Order," as discussed by Bohm and Peat, or in Laszlo's "*Vacuum Plenum* Field." In other words, there is a local correlation with non-local fields. The generative base is the archetype that then spins its influence through the creation of a corresponding field of attraction.

Perhaps a teleological dimension of fields concerns the psyche's attempt to make its contents known and accessible to the ego. We have a theological precedent for this speculation in the Judeo-Christian religious tradition, where humans are viewed as being created in the image of God. Here God is made manifest through incarnation into matter. Also, the Biblical reference to "the word made flesh" speaks to the psyche's ongoing attempts to find a material representation of its spiritual dynamics. Possibly this is also true for the relationship between the archetype, the archetypal field, and the individual.

The archetype creates its influence as if throwing out a high-powered radio signal accessible to everyone regardless of space and time considerations. Similar to the workings of radio stations, where each station plays a certain genre of music—jazz, rock, or classical—, archetypal frequencies emit their own specific material. Like the ever-present solar frequencies emitted by the earth itself, these archetypal forces affect everyone regardless of individual recognition. Here again we see the relevance of Becker and Lawrence Fagg's work on electromagnetic fields and my studies on archetypal fields.

FIELD, FORM, AND FATE

Symmetry Between Field and Form:
A Hand-and-Glove Fit Between Archetype and Form

Each species requires specific environmental conditions to ensure its survival. The mutability and adaptability of a species will enhance its likelihood of survival in an ever-changing world. However, in becoming excited about diversity, change, and complexity, we may sometimes forget that the conditions out of which complexity emerges begin with the activation of a replicative, non-complex regime. The human fetus develops through the process of replication and duplication of a single cell and follows a seemingly eternal, archetypal morphology in its movement from potential to form.

As discussed previously, each species follows its own archetypal and morphological currents in order to ensure a successful expression of its innate form, which lives *in potentia*, into a material substance. Alignment with these properties brings symmetry between individual and field. This symmetry and alignment carry a powerful archetypal effect that works to collapse individual experience into a morphological singularity. In other words, individual experience is temporally superseded by the workings of transpersonal archetypal fields that follow prefigured trajectories in their journey from potential to form.

A brief look at autonomous processes and their role in entraining individual expression with *a priori* archetypal, morphogenetic properties can also be understood within a spiritual context. In *Psychology and Religion,* Jung discusses the archetypal symbolism of the Roman Catholic Mass, explaining that this ritual has as its goal a reconnection to something divine, be it God or the Self. That to which we reconnect exists independent of consciousness. Through participation in the Mass:

> human consciousness (represented by the priest and congregation) is confronted with an autonomous event, which, taking place on a "divine" and "timeless" plane transcending consciousness, is in no way dependent on human action, but which impels man to act by seizing upon him as an instrument and making him the exponent of a "divine" happening. (*CW 11,* § 379)

Jung proceeds by suggesting that the Mass represents

> The manifestation of an order outside time [and] involves
> the idea of a miracle which takes place ... at the moment
> of transubstantiation . . . The ritual of the Mass takes
> this situation and transforms it step by step until the cli-
> max is reached—the Consecration, when Christ himself,
> as sacrificer and sacrificed, speaks the decisive words
> through the mouth of the priest. At that moment, *Christ
> is present in space and time.* (my italics, *CW 11*, § 307)

"Anamnesis" is the liturgical term given to what happens during
the Mass. The church believed that during the Benediction, Consecra-
tion, and Transubstantiation, where bread and wine are transformed
into the body and blood of Christ, we have the opportunity to enter
into this eternal sacrifice. While we may tend to view the ceremony as
a ritualistic re-enactment of an event from the past, the church
believes that this event is ongoing and that, under special conditions,
we gain access to this domain.

Another way to understand this idea is to imagine that we have
just walked onto the beach and are suddenly struck by the sound of
waves crashing, the smell of the sea air, the sight of deep, blue water, and
we achieve a genuine sense of well being. While we may have just
arrived at the beach, it has always been there, available for our apprehen-
sion. So too with anamnesis, the experience is always there. The individual
or the collective may then find a way to enter this domain.

In so many important ways, this idea parallels my work on fields
as preexistent domains that, like frequencies on the radio, can be tuned
into and accessed. However, I want to be clear in saying that these
states are not playthings to amuse and satisfy the whims of the ego.
Accessing the archetypal is not a game. It tends to occur spontane-
ously and is not a casual experience.

In conclusion, Jung comments on the incarnation and manifestation of the transpersonal in the Mass:

> Yet his [Christ's] presence is not a reappearance, and
> therefore the inner meaning of the consecration is not a

45

repetition of an event which occurred once in history,
but the revelation of *something existing in eternity, a
rending of the veil of temporal and spatial limitations
which separates the human spirit from the sight of the
eternal.* (my italics, *CW 11,* § 307)

As the Mass works to entrain a congregation into the mysteries
of the Self and the transpersonal, so too do archetypal fields. To this
F. David Peat adds:

> In reference to the Mass, you have the notion of the non-
> local in space and time becoming manifest locally and
> at a moment in time. So you are circling around some-
> thing very interesting about locality and non-locality;
> about non-local archetypes and about localized fields,
> about biological, localized energy and something else.
> (Personal communication)

Both collapse the duality between individual-collective and ego-
self and make accessing the transpersonal and archetypal possible. We
see in this example that replication also serves to usher in the eternal.

In seeing through dualities, we discover that we are living in an
interconnected universe. Jung makes obvious his views about this
underlying order and connection. So too does Mae-Wan Ho (1993), a
biophysicist who sees interconnectivity and coherence as the underlying principles guiding life. The world's greatest mystics, scholars,
and artists have all wrestled with the question "What is life?" Dr. Ho,
through her many years of studies in the laboratory and her sensibility
as an artist, has come to view life in terms of coherence—coherence
being the orchestration of many components into a unified whole.
One example of the artistry of coherence in the natural world is found
in Benard convection cells. As we boil water, we find that with the
increase in temperature, a series of lattice-like formations develop in
the bottom of the pan. Dr. Ho writes:

> ... all the cells in the pan are synchronized with respect
> to one another ... at phase transition, however they

begin to move cooperatively until all molecules are dancing together in cellular formations as though choreographed to do so. It is appropriate to refer to them as coherent structures which are dynamically maintained. (*The Rainbow and the Worm,* 39)

Becker's work (1990) on regenerative activity also calls for a revised theory of the whole and a recognition of the power of coherent patterns. He writes:

Obviously, the process of regeneration in the salamander must be completely related to the entire remainder of the organism by some energetic mechanism that encompasses and organizes the total organism in a fashion that cannot be explained by the chemical paradigm. To watch this miracle of limb regeneration occur is the most convincing evidence I know of for the awesome and still unknown power of life. (*Cross Currents,* 34)

One senses from these comments that we are on the verge of rediscovering what the mystics, alchemists, and poets have known for centuries—namely, the existence of an *unus mundus.* Our capacity to recognize patterns brings us into relationship with the archetypal. Patterns are the footprints of the divine, the imprints of the archetype, whose recognition and assimilation is transformative. I hope that in some small way this book shows how to make these reconnections and how, in realizing the presence of patterns and fields, we can engage more meaningfully with an underlying archetypal and spiritual reality.

CHAPTER THREE

An Archetypal Field Theory

The concept of self-organizing fields is finding increasing support and validation in diverse disciplines. Field theory and, in particular, my interests in the relationships among archetypes, patterns, and fields arise from a search for an understanding of archetypal processes and those forces responsible for the creation of life, the emergence of form, and the evolution of complexity in the human psyche and in the natural world.

For centuries we have tried to locate and identify the so-called elementary particle—the fundamental building block of material existence. With progressively advanced technology, we have discovered more than fifty of them, although some may be only different states of the same particle, and none may be truly elementary—that is, irreducible to simpler elements.

Even the idea that an elementary particle exists suggests our continued reliance on a mechanistic world view, which postulates that all events are deducible from their antecedents, according to the laws of nature. However, the results of our search have ironically paved the way for a conceptual revolution that is gradually eclipsing prevailing deterministic, causal paradigms.

As Gary Zukav (1979) explains, experiments in particle physics were initially designed in terms of traditional expectations. Particles were shot at one another to determine which elements would survive. These basic remaining elements would then be presumed to be "the ultimate building blocks of the universe." What happened, however, forced science to look at reality from another vantage point.

Zukav writes:

> When the projectile strikes the target, both particles are
> destroyed at the point of impact. In their place, however,
> are created new particles all of which are as elementary as
> the original particles and often as massive as the original
> particles . . . [In other words, every] subatomic interaction
> consists of the annihilation of the original particle and
> the creation of new subatomic particles. (*The Dancing
> Wu Li Masters*, 215)

Field theory offers a plausible explanation for these results.
It postulates that matter is the outcome and not the source of the
creative process.

> Fields alone are real. They are the substance of the uni-
> verse. Matter (particles) is simply the momentary
> manifestation of interacting fields which intangible and
> insubstantial as they are, are the only real things in the uni-
> verse. (*Dancing Wu Li Masters*, 219)

A significant implication of this hypothesis—that form and substance are the by-products of intangible interacting fields—is
supported by Jung's ideas about archetypal reality, ideas which were
once perceived as mystical. Jung described the archetypes as the psychological correlates of the instincts because they force human
perception and comprehension into specific patterns. He regarded the
images generated by the archetypes as the primordial, universal
thoughts of humanity, which exist independent of consciousness
and the will.

Jung understood that the archetype, like a field in the natural
world, is distinct from its observable derivatives and can be manifested in either the psychic or physical realm; that is, an archetypal
patterning organizes not only mental images and ideas but also material events. In fact, Jung speculated that psyche and matter are simply
two different aspects of the same thing. Consequently, he explained
synchronistic events, which are temporally related but causally dis-

tinct, as being connected by a common archetype. This view of the indivisibility of psyche and matter takes us into what Jung described as the psychoid realm. In many respects, this notion of the psychoid and its bridging of matter and psyche is the concept that allows for the confluence of Jungian psychology and the new sciences, since each speaks to an underlying, generative realm from which psyche and matter arise.

Today, Jung's ideas are echoed in other disciplines. For example, an expert in chaos theory, Robert Pool, in an article, entitled "Catching the Atom Wave" (*Science,* 1995) says:

> On a head scratching scale of 1 to 10, the notion that matter can act as both a particle and a wave rates at least a 9. This concept, central to quantum mechanics, has mystified people for decades, inspiring science fiction and sophomoric philosophizing. Physicists are not more comfortable with it than any one else, but they have learned to accept the weirdness and put it to work .... (1129)

The shift from an atomistic view of the world to a unified field theory is probably most apparent, at the popular level, in disciplines that were at a disadvantage under the old paradigm. For example, emerging theories of female development, such as those coming from the Stone Center Research Group at Wellesley College, suggest that the female psyche, rather than striving for autonomy and separation (traditional psychology's normative and male-oriented route to mature cognition and behavior), may develop instead in accordance with a different archetypal field, one emphasizing a greater degree of relatedness and connection. The point is not that this is a viable idea about feminine development, although it may be, but that paradigm shifts often work their way into popular consciousness by explaining experiences of reality that cannot be described by old frames of reference. The effects then become visible at both individual and collective levels.

The very premise that a generative field exists out of which matter is created has fueled a range of hypotheses that go beyond the pioneering work of Zukav and his colleagues. During a discussion at our 1992 Assisi Conference, Ervin Laszlo suggested that: "Fields predate the configuration of matter and ... matter emerges out of these prefigured, informational fields."

To put this in concrete terms, consider the fetus in the womb. The form a baby eventually develops may be said to exist even prior to the moment of conception. This is the same point Jung made in the psychological realm—archetypes are form *in potentia*, a type of structural shaping. Although classical biologists have attributed the appearance and development of form solely to the unfolding of DNA processes, they cannot definitively point to a chemical blueprint located in the DNA code that is responsible for the specificity of the myriad forms found in the human body. This suggests that the potential for form exists independent from temporal, interactional, biochemical dynamics, and its impetus remains relatively constant across a wide-ranging set of possibilities.

The notion of field preceding form is also captured in Arthur Conan Doyle's Sherlock Holmes short story "The Adventure of the Copper Beeches." The story begins with a wealthy landowner interviewing housekeepers for his country estate. After perhaps fifty interviews, he finds the one woman appropriate for the job. In their discussion, he explains her duties. At the conclusion of the interview, he confides a final and unusual job requirement. She must cut her long, beautiful hair into a carefully described style. After some resistance, she finally concedes and accepts the position. Once on the job, the landowner's wife tells the housekeeper that every afternoon at two o'clock she must also wear a particular dress and sit in the window seat for an hour, while the landowner regales her with tales and jokes.

Realizing how bizarre this situation is, the young woman calls on Sherlock Holmes for assistance. With his help she uncovers the true story. The landowners have banned their daughter from marrying her beloved and forced her to live in the tower room of their estate. To keep the daughter's lover from learning about her imprisonment, the parents have the new housekeeper assume the daughter's role. This serves to maintain the illusion of the daughter's presence in the family and perhaps also provides the parents a sense of joy, albeit delusional, of being with their daughter.

While the underlying plot is relatively easy to discern, I am nevertheless struck by how it illustrates that field precedes form. The parents had an image of their daughter that the new employee had to live into. The details of this enactment were very precise, down to the color and style of hair, the particular dress, the placement in the window seat, and the ritual of the two o'clock story-telling sessions. These conditions had to be met in order to fill and live out the underlying family drama.

We continue to discover more evidence of the power of fields to structure and influence the creation of form in the outer world. And, like in Arthur Conan Doyle's tale, the details of the form maintain a high degree of fidelity to the morphology of the field. However, one also needs to account for the process of change and the emergence of complexity in the life process. Robert Rosen addresses both of these aspects of systemic dynamics: "In some sense, the states represent what is intrinsic about a system, while the dynamical laws reflect the effects of what is outside or external" (324) David Bohm reached the same conclusion, as reflected in his theory of the implicate and explicate order, as did Jung, who distinguished between an energetic, archetypal field and its static expression in symbols and images.

The idea is also found in myth and religion, as often happens when scientific truths are beyond intellectual reach. For example, in the Bible's story of Creation, humanity is fashioned "in the image and likeness of God." Here again, we see the explication in matter of *a priori* form, which before its incarnation in flesh existed as a potentiality of psyche and spirit. These images speak to the idea that individual form emerges from a larger, autonomous, preexistent field, inaccessible to direct awareness.

In the psychological realm, this concept offers a fruitful way to understand psychodynamic issues that do not lend themselves to purely causal explanations. The standard approach to a client's disorder is essentially causal. Problematic behavior is explained by antecedent conditions in the client's life experience—an alcoholic parent, an abusive family situation, and so forth. Although one can make a case for causal determinants of behavior, this reductive approach presumes that conscious awareness of the early experience is the primary basis for cure.

Jung, on the other hand, posited that life patterns often begin at conception and that the resulting psychological and archetypal ambiance within an individual's life is an expression of these fields. For instance, in considering the life of someone who has been orphaned at birth and the ongoing dynamics of his or her experiences, we all too often find the drama of being orphaned as the dominant, ongoing theme throughout his or her life. From a cognitive and behavioral point of view, we easily can say that the individual continues to engage in activities that inevitably end in abandonment. However, archetypal field theory perhaps offers a more compelling perspective on these dynamics. Clearly, being orphaned is a trauma in that the individual enters the world with all the hopes for love and for the good enough parenting one "should have," only to find that for many different reasons, he or she is born into a death field. His or her earliest hopes for containment and love have been met with abandonment and loss. This is not meant to cast blame in any direction, but is instead an attempt to describe the psychological and archetypal landscape of the orphan experience.

Using a field approach, we clearly acknowledge that the conditions of conception and birth continue to play a pivotal role in the individual's life. However, we also recognize the archetypal, universal aspects of the experience, as reflected in the orphan archetype, and the striking similarity in behavior in the lives of orphans generally, who have been with us since the beginning of time. Perhaps the high degree of resonance in the behavior of individuals within this field speaks to the overarching, non-personal, *a priori* influence of this particular archetypal constellation whose properties exist as a preformed experience in human nature and have been conserved in

54

the psyche through countless iterations. So we can envision that as each individual is orphaned, he or she enters a preexistent, archetypal field associated with particular behaviors, influences, and tendencies. Next, we begin to view our therapeutic work as both an articulation and freeing of the individual from the iterative dynamics of the field.

Regardless of which field is activated, whether it involves children of alcoholic parents, orphans, etc., change is clearly possible. While the deep archetypal, morphological core of the orphan archetype will remain a central constellation within the individual's life, what can change is that he or she can establish an individual, highly differentiated response to it. In so doing, he or she can learn about the archetype's objective features and tendencies. For example, orphans, through the experience of having the security of the parental archetype shattered at birth, are more children of the Self and the deep unconscious than of the material, mother world. This often translates to their experiencing a high number of synchronistic experiences and having uncanny intuitive abilities.

Interestingly enough, fields often carry the seeds of one's future destiny. Edward Whitmont, a late Jungian analyst in New York, made a similar point:

> Relevant events in a patient's past history, which we have been in the habit of viewing as causes of current psychopathology, may now perhaps be seen as manifestations of the beginning life-pattern. Traumatic events of childhood ... may perhaps be seen as essential landmarks in the actualization of a pattern of wholeness, as the necessary "suffering of the soul" which engenders present and future psychological advance. ("The Destiny Concept in Psychotherapy," 186-87)

We can see how this idea plays out at the popular level in astrology, which posits that the conditions surrounding one's birth are a determining factor in the unfolding of one's destiny and fate.

Borrowing from Einstein, we can say that the problem with a reductive, causally based psychology is "not that its answers are wrong; only that its questions are too small." From this perspective, Freud's theory of repetition compulsion, as well as the more behaviorally driven explanations for repetitive behavior, offers only a partial explanation of replicative phenomena. If we understand that an individual is embedded in a specific archetypal field, his or her behaviors can be viewed as consistent features structured and patterned by the properties of that field. For example, do victims of incest, who frequently marry perpetrators or masochistic partners, do so because of their early experiences? Or is the family situation itself part of a larger field in which the child and later the adult remain caught?

Recent studies suggest that patients who have received organ transplants exhibit behaviors and traits of the unknown organ donor. From the perspective of field theory, we suggest that the transplanted body part remains connected to the donor's field, carrying with it, as does a hologram, a composite of the donor's characteristics and life experiences. So, even in death, the field of the donor may continue to exert its influence on the organ recipient. It may well be that field theory will help unify many of these kinds of anomalous events and situations, which are now considered unrelated.

Alex Andrews (1989), in a discussion of what is termed "ocular dominance," describes an experiment in which kittens' ocular nerves were surgically altered to insure either vertical or horizontal dominance. It was found that even after the effects of the early surgery were reversed, the kittens' visual cortices maintained the early visual dominance. He relates that: "Those reared with experiences only of vertical stripes would readily play with a pencil presented vertically but seemed blind to one proffered horizontally" (*Self Organizing Systems,* 77). Although one could offer a behavioral or neuropsychological explanation for the kittens' responses, one might also suggest that the experience of vertical or horizontal dominance carried a field of influence within which the kittens became embedded. Their behavior thus reflected the laws and properties belonging to that field.

When applied to psychological behavior, the notion of field-specific and field-generated responses has important implications. Lisa

Freden, a therapist in New England, suggests that when an individual remains embedded in a specific field—like an incest or alcoholic field—he or she becomes resistant to the influence of other, more diverse and complex fields. For example, studies have shown that individuals blind since birth have great difficulty adjusting to life if they gain their sight.

Fields may be viewed in this respect as the medium through which archetypes incarnate into matter. Dreams, symbols, synchronicities, somatic responses—are all manifestations of archetypal information. Surrounding every archetype is a symbol canon—the images and symbols from which an archetypal core may be inferred. These images reveal the essential, dominant, and unique features of the archetype from which they originate. In this sense, a symbol or image stands as an orientational marker, directing us to a specific, archetypal field.

For this reason, Jung's own manner of working with archetypal images was almost entirely objective. He determined the dominant, universal aspects of an archetypal image, traced their existence in collective materials worldwide, and attempted to understand the specific contexts in which the image appeared.

A client's associations and feelings about an image may reveal a great deal about its personal and relative significance as well as the client's personal alignment to the archetype. However, the objective and archetypal meaning of an image often cannot be derived from a client's feelings about it. The archetype remains deeply embedded in the natural world, and its essential nature is not altered by our individual orientation to it. Objective, universal, ontological characteristics of an image often remain obscured from individual consciousness. Consequently, if a client dreams, for instance, of a black bear, a therapist should consider not just the client's feelings and associations to the black bear, but also all those objective, natural traits that are specific to the bear (whether or not the client is consciously aware of them)—and not just any bear, but a black bear, which has evolved in its behavior and appearance to meet a particular set of environmental challenges.

Considering the innate properties of the symbol itself, rather than equating its meaning to a client's personal attitudes and biases toward it, gives the client an objective basis from which he or she can move beyond a limited, subjective framework. As Jung well understood, the conscious mind is only the surface of a teeming subterranean dimension of existence whose laws reflect the laws of nature, not the biases of the conscious mind, and must be respected.

There have been many occasions in my own practice when a client's dream contained an image neither the client nor I knew anything about. One such incident involved a dream about a lungfish. In order to discover the archetypal, non-personally derived meaning of the image, I called the Boston Aquarium to get as much information as I could about the lungfish. I found out that the lungfish is unique in its ability to survive for long periods of time out of water by burrowing in the mud. This characteristic revealed a great deal about the patient's own capacity to endure the long process of therapy and the hardships of life. The psyche thus conveyed a message with precisely the right image. The patient's personal associations to fish or to lungs in general would not have provided this insight, which reflected the archetypal underpinnings of the patient's life.

The specificity of imagery and its power to influence is amusingly captured in the play *Fiddler on the Roof*. Much of the play concerns the struggle to integrate new ideas into a traditional framework of assumptions, beliefs, and expectations. One of these "new ideas" is that romantic love can be the foundation for marriage. Tevye and Golde have arranged a marriage between their daughter Tzeitel and the aged butcher Lazar Wolf. But Tzeitel has already fallen in love with the tailor Motel. Tevye needs to convince Golde to accept their daughter's decision. He reasons that if someone as important and influential as Golde's deceased grandmother appears in a dream to champion the tailor's cause, his wife will be more likely to view the marriage as divinely sanctioned.

So Tevye feigns a dream in which the grandmother returns. Golde says that if her beloved grandmother took the trouble to come all the way back from the grave to deliver this message, then so be it. Tzeitel will marry the tailor. The ghostly image carried with it a specific moral, spiritual, and cultural imperative that Golde felt obliged to obey. Had Tevye dreamed instead of the village beggar, the image would have had a different impact.

In this same way, every image the psyche offers carries with it unique, archetypal, moral, spiritual, and psychological mandates and imperatives. The meaning of one image cannot be confused with the meaning of another, even within a similar domain. A black bear is, quite simply, not a polar bear.

One of the current trends in the field of depth psychology is the increasing reliance on constructivist and cognitive approaches to symbols and to personal experience. Such approaches emphasize the subjective dimension of a client's psyche. As these views become normative, the distinction Jung made between archetypal and personal material is ignored along with our capacity to heed the autonomous wisdom of the psyche. Although conscious and subjective dynamics may bring an archetype into play, an archetypal image is not simply reducible to consciously derived meanings and may in fact be at odds with them.

Archetypal fields, like morphogenetic fields, contain the information necessary for generating and sustaining form. As Laszlo, one of the world's greatest systems theorists and a pioneer in the new sciences suggests, form as we know it emerges out of fields, and the information contained therein is converted into matter. In a recent paper, Laszlo extends this idea into the arena of world history. He attributes the ongoing disregard and destruction of human life to our overvaluing of individualism, which results ultimately in the need to destroy what is perceived as alien. He believes that the glorification of individualism extracts as its price our inability to understand the underlying unity and interconnectedness of life, which is a far more fundamental and primary state of existence.

We can see this deification of the subjective as subsidizing the above-mentioned theories of constructionism and the general movement in Self Psychology, which speak to the singular value of individual experience and personal will. Remember, however, that Jung encouraged dialogue between the individual and the objective psyche. To proceed with this preempting of the Self and the objective psyche and to continue making a false god of the ego is terribly costly. The price of such a limitation is profound, as we see in our continuing collective march towards global destruction. The hope for peace, which is perhaps ultimately unreachable, is sustained by our sense of relationship with others.

I recall watching a recent news report of troops shipping out in preparation for a Middle East war. Soldiers were saying tearful goodbyes to their wives, husbands, children, and other loved ones. The outpouring of emotion was contagious, and I too felt a deep sense of pain in thinking that these soldiers might never again see their children and families. While war ultimately may help to bring about peace, it is done at the loss of many lives. To defend against this pain, the archetype of war entrains its players into its own spin, with one of the central characteristics being the need to heartlessly kill the enemy. Could we so easily take another human life if we had to think about the other's personal, familial situation? Also, with the ecological and eco-psychology movements, we find a deep connection to the environment, realizing that we are part of an ongoing dance where we affect and are affected by the earth.

I believe that an investigation into the workings of archetypal fields and the development of an archetypal field theory may help to compensate for our culture's increased disregard for psychic autonomy, the wisdom of nature, and the role of unseen forces in the individual and collective psyche. The wisdom of the elders, who taught about the *Unus Mundus*, is again being heard as a whisper, a *sottovoce*. Perhaps we can find some modern amphitheater within which to amplify and listen to this message of underlying unity between individuals and between matter and psyche.

CHAPTER FOUR

Archetypal Patterns

O ver the past five years, I have developed an increasing respect and awareness of patterns in the natural world. Patterns exist in every facet of life, and through the intricate, fascinating, and beautiful designs they assume, we can see the high degree of self-organization, complexity, and stability working to create them. Consider the very organized patterns and designs found in seashells, in the plumage of birds, and in the human body itself. Within the camps of biophysics, biology, and mathematical biology, patterns are often understood as the species' attempt to insure survival. The pivot point in many of these interpretative efforts hangs on the notion of adaptability and the survival value of ornamentation in animals. Thus the presence of beautiful feathers on a bird is seen as nature's way of insuring the attractability of one member of the species to another and assisting in the continuance and survival of the species.

However, back in the 1950s, the work of Adolf Portmann, a biologist, colleague of Jung, and long-standing contributor to the Eranos Conferences, proved that in many cases colorful plumage in birds has no survival value. Based upon these observations, he proposed that every organism simply lives with a mandate to express its natural and unique characteristics. In moving beyond the prevailing Darwinian paradigm, Portmann offers a fascinating and meaningful bridge to Jung's view that the Self is constantly striving for expression. Patterns, for Portmann, were expressions of an animal's interrelationship and interconnection with the natural world and of the innate nature of the animal itself. Patterns also revealed what stage of life the animal was in. Through ornamentation and melodic song, we hear the telling of a bird's life story, and, in the telling, the story is heard by other members of the species.

In the realm of relationships, we also find that couplings are much more highly organized into recognizable archetypal patterns than one might imagine. For instance, the relationship of a married couple may resemble the troubled, mythical relationship of Echo and Narcissus. In this regard, the couple's behaviors and tendencies are essentially archetypal in nature and are governed by the dominants and traits found in the Echo/Narcissus archetypal constellation. In such instances, the personal domain of choice and conscious differentiation has been lost, thus producing a life lived out on an archetypal, not a human, level. In a fascinating, yet often tragic, way, the fate of individuals caught in such transpersonal couplings often parallels the eternal dramas described in myths about these archetypal figures.

We also find archetypal couplings and patterns operative in the teacher-student relationship, the client-therapist relationship, and in the business world, where each evolves in accordance with a pre-formed, archetypal morphology. At first glance, one looks either at the physical world or at relationships and sees a loosely knit set of dynamics, imagining that they result from a random combination of events. However, upon examination, one finds a high degree of coherence and order. For instance, while all seashells contain individual differences, they are still structured in accordance with a set of morphogenetic constants that account for their symmetry and underlying design.

Human relationships also tend to be structured and informed by specific archetypal fields. These fields are evidenced in relationships through the presence of patterned behaviors and role evocation between members. We can thus speak of father-daughter or mother-son archetypal couplings. Individuals embedded within a field maintain a high degree of consistency and entrainment to the ontology of the constellated archetype. As the compelling power of the archetype takes hold and absorbs personal consciousness, the individual or couple's behavior and interactional patterns remain refractory to attempts to break the symmetry established by the archetype, thus further subsidizing the possession.

In the treatment relationship, we also find fairly well defined, patterned couplings occurring between client and therapist even in the initial interview. For the sensitive observer, these couplings become increasingly more obvious and interesting, further demonstrating the power of fields to orchestrate interactional and lifelong patterns. Additionally, we realize that virtually every human interaction and experience is an externalization and incarnation of an archetype into space and time.

St. Francis and many of the early mystics viewed matter as the imprint of the divine making itself known in the outer world. This perspective helps us develop an even greater appreciation of matter. Every living thing becomes manifest in the world through a spacio-temporal representation in matter. The emergent properties of matter proceed from potential to form in correspondence to a set of archetypal, morphological regularities.

The human body exists as the matter equivalent and manifestation of DNA information, which has been translated into form. Only slight variations exist between the DNA of an ape and a human. Each DNA code has a corresponding morphological, nascent form, which will, in virtually every instance, appear in the material world in a highly stable configuration. The ape will have ape-like features, and the human, human features. Let's take this one step further and look at the minuscule difference between the DNA composition of the general population and that of Downs Syndrome children. The slight variation in the DNA of Downs Syndrome children produces a design unique to them. The emergent form is already preformed and has then gone through the transition and translation from potential to form through the conversion of information and archetypal potentialities into matter.

We find that each component part of a field, like the individual parts of the body, is expressive and representative of an overarching pattern within which each part is embedded. From the singular appearance of virtually any part of the body, like the nose, we can infer that it is contained within a larger picture, namely, the face. In this regard, we can appreciate how archetypal and morphogenetic fields express their characteristic form through the stabilization of patterns and require exacting symmetry and coherence.

Central to the emergence of life is the finding that almost all systems contain inhibitors and enhancers. Enhancers ensure the successful growth of the organism, while inhibitors keep growth patterns within the parameters of the system's underlying morphology. Height in men and women generally falls within a predetermined range. Enhancers ensure that a height within the range is reached, while inhibitors ensure that the range is not exceeded. The human body as a system responds to a set of periodic attractors, which govern many functions such as heart rate, blood pressure, height, and weight. Interestingly enough, the absence of either an enhancer or an inhibitor is often injurious to the system. In the case of gigantism, or even when looking at the uncontrolled proliferation of cancer cells, we notice the absence of an inhibitory function. In both cases, growth continues uncontrollably, as the organism keeps responding to an unending series of prompts by enhancers. In fact, a recent radio report discussed a relatively new cancer treatment where shark cartilage is used as an inhibiting agent to the uncontrolled growth of cancer cells. All of the above suggest that the stabilization of form makes the task of identifying the underlying archetype and its morphology a more discernible and less daunting task.

Important information is holographically encoded in the minute details of one's life. Although I wrote my doctoral dissertation on the initial interview close to fifteen years ago, I am only now beginning to realize that my primary interest was in the holographically encoded archetypal information that tends to be expressed in highly stabilized patterns. In comprehending the interactional patterns that are established, even at the moment the client decides to begin treatment, the therapist gains access to a wealth of material. The details of the initial phone conversation often reveal the properties of the archetypal pattern in which the patient and the therapist are embedded. This way of understanding patterns is similar to Freud's ability to make fairly reliable clinical assessments based upon his client's relationships to money and sex. His observations about the phallic and anal personality types remain a valuable diagnostic yardstick. In observing, for instance, the client's tendency to hoard money, Freud realized that an anal-retentive quality, or pattern, permeated the individual's life and served as a type of periodic attractor, drawing to it only self-similar experiences, evidenced in particular sexual, financial, and emotional tendencies.

The power of fields and their tendency toward self-iteration/replication result in the client-therapist dyad organizing around a set of archetypal regularities. For instance, in treating a client with a history of incest, we often find a reactivation of incest boundary problems—a boundary violation, or transgression, inevitably occurs in the interactions between client and therapist. The influence of the archetypal field, in this instance the victim field, works to entrain both members of the therapeutic dyad into alignment with the personal trauma, which remains essentially archetypal in nature. This creates an interactional field whose properties and dynamics recapitulate and provide a new edition of the personal and archetypal constellation.

However, rather than viewing these interactions from the perspective of transference-countertransference, I find it more accurate to say that the psyche draws and entrains both the client and therapist into a synchronized, entrained pattern where their collective behavior reveals the nature of the activated archetype. In this regard, one can read the field in reverse in that the details of the relationship provide a picture of the constellated archetype. I am consistently struck by the stabilization of form within these archetypal configurations and the fidelity with which the client-therapist dyad reenacts the tenets of both the personal past and the archetypal field within which each person is embedded. The following is an illustration of how these fields may be expressed in the initial interview and how the conditions of treatment serve to constellate and stabilize these dynamics.

Case Vignette

The initial intake notes, taken by a secretary at the mental health center where Julie, a therapist, worked, indicated that individual appointments had been made for both members of a couple, whom we will call Mary and Bill. Having previously explained to the clinical and administrative staff her disinterest in seeing couples or members of the same family, Julie questioned the secretary as to how and why these appointments had been made. Bill was scheduled for an appointment the same day that Julie found these notes so that she was unable to contact him, cancel the appointment, and refer him elsewhere.

Bill arrived for his session twenty to thirty minutes late. He apologized, explaining that he had driven like a madman to get there. Right away, Julie noticed an aristocratic, if not pompous, feigned sense of self importance about him, similar to that described in Helena Deutch's "As if personality profile." She also sensed a certain shiftiness and possible psychopathic potential. Unable to properly manage her own anxieties, Julie brought Bill into the consulting room and immediately explained that she did not do couples counseling and would not be able to treat him. She went on to tell him what had been written about him on the intake form and, in so doing, revealed that his wife was scheduled for an interview later that week with her.

While I believe it was a violation to inform Bill about his wife's appointment, since it was possible that it was intended to be a private consultation and was perhaps even a secret from him, I find it meaningful that the initial interview was so chaotic. Bill explained that he and his wife wanted couples therapy and that he was disappointed the therapist was not available, since she had been highly recommended. Then he became quite flirtatious with her. She correctly saw his seductive behavior as a derivative, unconscious expression about the nature of his psyche and about the confused conditions of treatment, where a triangulation and betrayal had already occurred.

Bill was sent back to the intake coordinator, who upon his urging, called his wife Mary to clarify her requests and needs for treatment. Mary quickly explained that she was seeking individual treatment, was already separated from her husband, and in fact had begun divorce proceedings—information the husband hid from the therapist.

Arriving for her session with Julie later in the week, Mary explained that while she had suspected her husband's infidelity for some time, it was recently confirmed when he "mistakenly" left a note from his lover on the kitchen table. Mary confronted him and told him that she planned to leave him. Bill became verbally abusive and tried to prevent her from ending the marriage. Fearing that his verbal assaults would escalate into physical violence, she consulted a lawyer and obtained a restraining order against him in an effort to protect herself. She was also anxious about her husband's upcoming trip home (outside the United States), where he would be accompanied by their two children, ages seventeen and thirteen. She was afraid that he would not return the children to her. Coupled with his continued disloyalties and betrayals, her concerns were certainly justified. Equally disquieting were Mary's fears that her husband would become violent, fears that were strangely reminiscent of what had recently happened to her two sisters (i.e. both had been beaten and repeatedly raped by their husbands). Mary also explained that while her parents had not been physically abusive to her as a child, they were still often on the verge of losing control. What was striking in this clinical episode was the degree of fidelity and consistency in Mary's current experiences in her marriage, in the traumatic occurrences in her two sisters' marriages, and in the highly conflicted events surrounding the beginning of the treatment relationship.

Much of my research on the initial interview matches the thinking of dynamical systems theorists who posit that the steady state of a system often reveals both its past, and occasionally even its potential, future states. "The Fournier Transform" is a mathematical formulation that suggests that a system's history is contained in its wave function. To illustrate how this works, imagine the two following scenarios. In the first case, we see a body of water and notice a particular wave formation. The waves are of a certain height and strength heading in a northeasterly direction. In the second case, we have much larger waves heading in the opposite direction. An oceanographer or others skilled at reading the ocean, like Polynesian sailors, could tell what sort of boat produced which waves and could also provide minute details as to the speed of the boat, its direction, and how long ago it had traveled on the waterway. The waves and the system's steady state are incredibly rich in information. However, while the Fournier Transform informs us about the system's past, we can also make reliable inferences about the system's potential future states. I suggest that if the current steady state in treatment is not interrupted by a perturbation as strong as that of the original pattern, it may proceed endlessly into the future. Thus we have the workings of replicative phenomena.

Many colleagues, including Fred Abraham, Ervin Laszlo, F. David Peat, and Peter Saunders, have challenged my position regarding the need for a high level perturbation to evoke change in the therapeutic situation. They state that in dynamic systems, change often results from small, rather than large, perturbations. However, my investigations in the clinical domain indicate that the human psyche, when embedded in a specific, archetypal alignment and field, remains much more refractory to change than other systems in the natural world and tends to require larger perturbations to promote change. The reason is that for the human psyche to change, it must find a way to tolerate the breakdown of various denial structures that remain repressed while the replicative regime is in force. We are talking about moving the system by way of third state, informational catastrophes: the perturbation introduces highly divergent material to which the system has to respond either by adaptation and integration or through the strengthening of its denial structures.

The unfolding of events in this clinical situation reveals a series of high-level perturbations:

1) The therapist was asked to have individual sessions with both members of the couple.

2) The therapist's request not to see couples or to treat members of the same family had been ignored.

3) The husband arrived late for the session.

4) The husband had made an appointment for both himself and his wife in order to avoid individual counseling that had been the condition for any possible reconciliation.

5) The therapist decided not to treat the husband.

6) The therapist called the wife to tell her about the interview with the husband and her decision to refer them elsewhere for couples counseling.

7) The wife's response that she wanted individual treatment and not couples counseling.

8) The wife's revelation on the phone that she was already separated from her husband.

As we continue the investigation into the emergence of form in these clinical interviews, we find the following details especially significant:

-The wife's discovery of the note from her husband's mistress.

-Her decision to end the marriage prompted by the husband's betrayal.

-The tragic events in her sisters' marriages.

-The wife's fears for her and her children's lives.

As I have described in other writings, the therapeutic situation serves as a stable attractor site, drawing to it material that resonates with the core of the constellated archetype. In this regard, the events and details emerging within the therapeutic dyad are essentially transpersonal in that the psyche works to entrain all members of the therapeutic enterprise into a synchronized alignment to the archetype.

When looking at the details of these interviews, particularly Mary's, we can hear that her unconscious communications were descriptive of the treatment experience, her marriage, and her life in general. Similarly, the clinician unconsciously exhibited her own dynamics when, for instance, she told Bill that she preferred not to work with him and failed to elicit his unconscious communications about the situation. Additionally, when she told him about his wife's upcoming appointment, she betrayed a confidence, and I believe she used this information as a way to evacuate her own anxiety about the case. While the situation was clearly complicated, and I understand the clinician's desire not to keep secrets from the husband, in this case it represented a betrayal of the wife's privacy.

The wife's material was even more striking in illustrating the degree of replication and entrainment found in her personal life, the conditions in therapy, and her family's past. Initially, her comments about being separated from her husband and wanting to have private treatment came as a surprise to the therapist and suggested that her interview was meant to be separate from the husband. References to the husband's infidelity and her decision to end the marriage triggered by his affair can be heard as her unconscious perceptions about the triangulation between the therapist, her husband, and herself that already existed in the treatment relationship.

The story about the husband seeing another woman is a clear unconscious derivative about the therapist's involvement as a third party in this imbroglio. Mary's unconscious may be suggesting that, like the presence of a third party—her husband's lover—in her marriage, therapy also involves a triangulation, and the therapist, whom she had hoped to have as her own, is on some important level already aligned with her husband. Even though Julie referred Bill to another therapist, I sense that the strength of the triangulation continued and jeopardized her ability to align herself with Mary. Additionally, Mary's reference to the note from Bill's lover indirectly comments on the therapist's reading the content of the intake notes to Bill, which inappropriately revealed her upcoming appointment with his wife. On one level, it was poor therapeutic judgment to have revealed this information. However, on a purposive level, perhaps there was a need to recreate and bring to life the underlying archetypal morphology within the therapeutic relationship so that the issue surfaced immediately. In this regard, we find that a central mandate of all living systems is the compelling need to find a corresponding expression in form and matter.

ARCHETYPAL PATTERNS

As Jung describes the archetypes' expression through symbols, so too is every relationship—be it a marriage, the therapeutic dyad, or a corporate structure—expressive of an underlying, archetypal dynamic. This way of viewing the relationship between the archetype and the natural world is strikingly Franciscan in that the world and its creations are taken as expressive of some autonomous force and influence, be it the Self or the divine. So too it seems that relationships and all aspects of matter express archetypal properties.

The wife's story about her sisters' tragic marriages reveals yet another level of derivative communication about the treatment. In the therapist's disclosures, coupled with the highly charged quality already present within the therapeutic environment, Mary's unconscious correctly perceived the dangerous elements in the treatment. In many respects, the story about the sisters' rapes represents Mary's unconscious perceptions of the treatment. Her marriage, her sisters' marriages (and as she later revealed her own family of origin), were filled with betrayals, lack of safety, and psychological violence. It seems that the treatment environment may have also lacked the security and understanding needed to help Mary break out of the cycle and life patterned on this theme of violence.

The main purpose in presenting this case is to illustrate the relationships that exist among an individual's internal archetypal orientation, its expression in his or her current life situation, and the events that unfold in the therapeutic relationship. It is as if the events occurring in Mary's life, her sisters' marriages, her family of origin, and now in therapy, unfolded in accordance with a blueprint that appears to be archetypal in nature. As in Laszlo's comment that matter and form are prefigured in fields, life appears to be organized in response to a preformed archetypal schema. Psyche has found a highly organized and precise way to manifest its inherent morphology within individual and collective life. Similar to carrier seashells which draw to them discarded debris from the ocean floor in an attempt to complete an inherent, preformed morphology, so too does the psyche go about casting relationships in an essentially impersonal and

71

transpersonal manner and organizing the events within them to express underlying archetypal dynamics. In the similarity of events that have occurred in different areas of Mary's life, we see how life often emerges in response to the presence of stable and, one can also add, reiterative attractors, whose morphology is so strong that from virtually any vantage point—be it her marriage or the events in treatment—one can infer the overarching field within which she is embedded. The notion that information about the whole can be holographically inferred from its parts can also be applied here.

The relationship can be viewed as a stage upon which the psyche presents a prearranged drama whose component parts are archetypal yet need the individuals to carry out their respective roles. While some may find this emphasis on the transpersonal orchestration of relationships disturbing, my findings in the clinical domain, in personal relationships, and in many social and cultural dynamics reveal that personal consciousness and differentiation actually play a far lesser role in the creation and movement of relationships, especially in their initial stages of formation, than we might think. Clearly, however, for growth and meaning to occur, one has to recognize the degree of archetypal entrainment taking place within a system and develop a differentiated response to these archetypal pulls. By doing so, one can learn the meaning of the particular archetypal field in which one is embedded.

It also must be explicitly stated that in order for the archetypal unfolding to occur, the therapist must be entrained to a particular archetypal constellation. In this example, the therapist's own life revealed a background that, while not as dramatic and violent as the couple's, had enough elements in common with it to allow for the entrainment.

Seeing the strength of the field of violence, as evidenced both by the circumstances of the client's life and the unfolding of events in treatment, I recommended that the therapist address all of these issues and discuss the possibility of referring the client to another therapist. Hopefully, in less replicative, chaotic conditions, a greater degree of safety might be experienced in the client's deep unconscious. While the client could view the referral as yet another betrayal, I sensed that this intervention would hopefully assist the client by:

1) Helping to identify the nature of the personal and archeypal field within which she, her family, and now the treatment, are embedded.

2) Offering her an opportunity to shift alignments from her current archetypal field to a more benevolent field and, in doing so, have, perhaps for the first time, an experience of relative safety. This may be initially accomplished by the therapist taking responsibility and being the one to articulate the dynamics of the client-therapist field. The strength of the entrainment may also help to successfully resolve the problem if the issues can be correctly metabolized and worked through both by the therapist and client.

The final point I want to address is the notion of individual change within the therapeutic process. If a realignment occurs, it will still be against the archetypal backdrop of the dominant field within which the individual's life has been cast. While therapeutic change and an archetypal realignment can occur in treatment, they still never undo the facts of one's life and past. I recall receiving a brochure in the mail years ago announcing a workshop, entitled "Redoing Our Childhood." We can make dramatic and meaningful changes in our lives, but we cannot and will never change the actual facts of our beginnings. A contrary attitude, such as that suggested by the workshop, reflects a glorified view of the ego's capabilites and reveals our collective denial of the immutable features of life, such as birth, birth order, death, and our origins.

Interestingly enough, we find in the lives of many of our creative, artistic, and cultural giants traumatic origins. While personally devastating and troubling, the actual role and impact of trauma may have to be re-evaluated when viewed through a teleological and archetypal lens.

The predominance of these original fields functions in ways that are similar to those set forth in the astrological view, where one's time of birth casts him or her within a specific and enduring constellation that continually exerts its influence throughout life. However, the therapeutic task can help break the archetypal possession of a field, and, as greater differentiation is achieved, the archetypal range of alignments available to the individual expands. For instance, while individuals born into the orphan field may tend to replicate the experience of abandonment in virtually every facet of their lives, our hope is to free them from the possessive hold of this archetype. Thus the individual remains an orphan but does not have to continually re-experience the ravages of abandonment, betrayal, and death.

The need to identify patterns is important in virtually every profession and facet of life. When treating a patient, the physician looks for a clustering of symptoms to aid in diagnosis and treatment. The symptom is usually part of a larger clustering of related symptoms that, as they form a recognizable pattern, become identified as a specific syndrome or disease. An example is found in Fisher's *Diseases of Infancy and Childhood* (1907), which describes the symptomatology of *pneumonia gastrica.*

> This form of the disease is one in which the symptoms of vomiting and diarrhea predominate, and hence it is known as the gastric type of pneumonia. While the lungs will show the usual symptoms of a croupous pneumonia, the tongue, stomach, and bowels will present symptoms of an intense inflammatory condition of the digestive tract. Not infrequently jaundice may be present. The conjunctival mucous membrane may be pigmented from the presence of bile. The secretions may also show biliary pigmentation. Herpes may appear on the upper lip, thus showing that there is an intense inflammatory condition affecting primarily the digestive tract. (*Diseases of Infancy and Childhood,* 499)

This elaborate description speaks to the degree of specificity and self-organization inherent in an internal condition like gastric pneumonia. Its particular characteristics are converted into matter and manifested in bodily symptoms. It is important for the clinician to develop observational skills and the ability to make the connection between a specific clustering of symptoms and the matrix or field out of which they are generated. In medical emergencies, a life can be saved by the clinician's ability to recognize and interpret accurately a patient's symptoms.

In the analytic domain, we also find a high degree of consistency between the properties of the archetypal field in which a client is embedded and his/her specific symptomatology. I have spent a number of years studying the patterns generated by the *"Puer-Puella Aeternus"* archetypal field, popularly known as the Peter Pan Syndrome, as they appear in the analytic relationship and the individual's life. While there are degrees of variation in the manifestations of this archetypal state, a core group of symptoms and issues still exists. These characteristics are discussed in Marie-Louise von Franz's classic work on the subject, *Puer Aeternus: A Psychological Study of the Adult Struggle with the Paradise of Childhood*, and include a general dissatisfaction with cultural and collective values, a sense of continual unrest, and a morbid fascination with death. In treatment, a similar clustering of issues arises that often center on the client's negative reactions and distaste for the frustrations and limitations on the conditions of treatment proposed by the therapist.

It is through these patterns that the analyst learns about various archetypal configurations and what life issues need to be addressed to facilitate healing. Similarly, the physician looks to recognizable patterns to determine the most appropriate treatment for a patient.

Discussions with Ervin Laszlo helped me clarify a number of points regarding the relationship between patterns and informational fields. Before, I had viewed the pattern as an autonomous entity emerging from the archetypal field, serving to influence a particular sequence of events and resulting in a configuration of form. However, Laszlo explained that the pattern, which can change, is a manifestation of the information contained within a field and is not, in and of itself, autonomous. It is an expression of the field.

In many respects, Laszlo's distinction between patterns and informational fields parallels Jung's understanding of the relationship between symbol and archetype. The pattern, like the symbol, emerges from an archetypal context, standing as a representation and "settling" into the form of the field. Both views logically attribute the generation of the original information represented in the form of a pattern to the source—the archetypal informational field.

Many of the interactional dynamics established between the client and therapist are influenced by archetypal fields. A specific pattern is often apparent in the client's initial phone call to the therapist. It unfolds through the questions he or she asks the clinician and the special conditions of treatment he may request. Similarly, many of the clinician's responses and initial interventions are representative of the field and its informational equivalent. In this light, we do well to reconsider our understanding of transference and countertransference phenomena. We can look at these operations as the unfolding of a field whose powerful influence draws both members of the therapeutic dyad, often unknowingly, into its purposeful spin, thus maintaining the pattern.

There are a number of disturbing implications and possible abuses associated with this perspective on field theory and its role in the therapeutic situation. The most dangerous misinterpretation may be a therapist's feeling justified in abandoning all clinical discretion and becoming involved in highly questionable and potentially injurious therapeutic behavior under the rationale that the "field made me do it." Such an attitude is abusive and destructive and could be grounds for charges of professional malpractice.

On the contrary, I am suggesting an approach to treatment in which the therapist makes interventions grounded in his/her best clinical judgment based upon years of training and supervision. And it is especially important that the interventions made match with an equal degree of specificity what is generated by the archetypal field.

CHAPTER FIVE

Replicative Patterns
An Archetypal Perspective

For the past ten to eighteen years, I have been investigating the dynamics of the initial interview and the beginning phase of therapy, which in many respects offer an important vantage point from which to understand the eventual evolution and trajectory that the therapeutic system will assume. As with the holographic model, we find that the whole is embedded and can be inferred from its parts. Thus seemingly insignificant details, such as the client's request for a reduction in fee or to bring additional members of his or her family into treatment—virtually any issue related to the therapeutic frame and the conditions of treatment—are, in fact, quite meaningful. These requests are part of a highly textured tapestry, with each thread an expression of the picture waiting *in potentia* to be revealed. As we find from related investigations into systems theory and human development, it is essential to identify the system's initial conditions. However much we struggle to isolate and name these original conditions, though, we must remember that there will always be a number of unidentified factors, or, as David Bohm terms these subtle influences, "hidden variables," which effect the system's evolution or devolution. Additionally, whatever initial conditions prevail, the system will inevitably enter a non-periodic, chaotic phase in its development.

FIELD, FORM, AND FATE

Clinical Vignette

The following clinical vignette illustrates a number of points about patterns and archetypally driven fields. The case involves a thirty-six-year-old woman Jean, in her fourth year of treatment with a senior analyst. At the time of the dream, Jean was applying for a postgraduate degree in the mental health field, which represented, among other things, an important step in the realization of a goal she had had for years. While she was preparing her application material and for the interview with the training board, she had this dream:

> I want to move to the Upper East Side of Manhattan. I find this beautiful two-bedroom apartment, with a great view of the city. I am very pleased and surprised to hear that the rent is only four hundred dollars per month. I quickly sign the lease and go out to celebrate.

This dream helps to illustrate the role of patterns, archetypal informational fields, Jung's idea of the dominant, and the clinical application of an archetypally driven field theory. In the opening of the dream, the theme of moving appears. Assessing Jean's associations to her dream images, we see that they capture her desire to improve her life psychologically and professionally, which is most likely reflected in her waking life in her applying to graduate school. The Upper East Side of Manhattan signifies a type of upscale living that she differentiated from the bohemian quality of New York's Upper West Side.

In the dream she is quite pleased and prepared to pay the rent of four hundred dollars per month. She knew that in reality one would pay between one to two thousand dollars for such an apartment. (The dream occurred in 1985, a time when the real estate market was booming in New York, resulting in exorbitant rental fees.)

When asked about the four hundred dollar rental fee, Jean explained that this figure might be realistic for an apartment in a run-down section of the city or in a shared housing arrangement, but not for a nice apartment on the Upper East Side, like the one in the dream. The celebration at the end of the dream obviously speaks to her excitement over signing the lease and of her imminent plans to move into the new apartment.

This material reflects the client's conscious associations to her dream images. The therapeutic and interpretative task involves finding the consonance or dissonance between these subjective, personal associations and their archetypal backdrop. The image, as with any manifestation of form, carries with it a holographically encoded snapshot of the entire informational field within which it is embedded. This point may be understood by further examining the dream.

Possibly the most striking and dissonant feature in this dream involves the unrealistically low rental price. If this situation were viewed solely from a subjective perspective, one would be excited, and indeed fortunate, with such a find. However, in viewing the image against its historical and archetypal background, it becomes relativized, and we find that a different story emerges.

Part of the archetypal dominant involved in finding housing is the need to find a way of life that is constructive and, equally important, one that can be afforded. In other words, finding a life that one can live in. The ability to assess what one can afford psychologically and financially is also an essential component of this archetypal background, part of the particular field that we will call the "finding a home" field. Here, money, both as a symbol and as material reality, speaks to the amount of psychological energy available or that needs to be generated by the individual to accomplish a goal. While we may want a beautiful home on a hundred acres in the country or a lovely upscale East Side apartment, we must assess our psychological and financial resources at the moment the particular expenditure is being questioned. While it is essential to have aspirations beyond our current capabilities, it is equally important to understand what it takes to acquire our dreams.

This method of working with the material may appear a bit constrictive and could easily lead one to think that if one's current situation were the only yardstick from which to judge the realization of goals, then I would be guilty of smothering my client's dreams and aspirations. On the contrary, I am suggesting that every event and situation is rooted in an archetypal field (here the housing field), wherein the habits or laws operative in the field have to be honored and engaged with to metabolize the information contained therein. Rather than crushing or dampening one's dreams, this approach offers a type of educational experience about archetypal realities and can help the client learn what particular situations and aspirations require in terms of psychological and financial expenses.

The monthly fee of four hundred dollars is out of line with what the real estate market bore for a two-bedroom apartment in 1985. The fee is roughly one-quarter of the market price. In recognizing and understanding this dissonance, we are in a position to make a number of important speculations about the dreamer.

The dream occurs in response to an important event in the dreamer's life—her application to the postgraduate school. The application process represents a temporal event on which the dream will comment. However, it also reflects a spacio-temporal manifestation of a larger, archetypal life pattern. In other words, Jean's responses to this particular situation will most likely reflect her relationship to the larger issue of investment and the capacity, financially and psychologically, to afford various things in her life. The overall pattern is holographically encoded in the current situation.

The situation thus carries important information for Jean about how to understand and navigate the archetypal field of investment. The events in life—such as buying a house or applying to a graduate program—are manifestations and incarnations of this theme in the outer world. Each individual experience emerges from a similar archetypal field, potentially offering the individual a better understanding of the various archetypal requirements established by nature and reinforced culturally for successful completion of this important life task.

The dissonance in the dream suggests that the dreamer is embedded in an archetypal pattern in which she is seriously unprepared and unaware of the psychological and archetypal expenditures required to accomplish her life goals. In light of the dreamer's awareness of the discrepancy between the rental fee in the dream and the actual cost of such an apartment, we have to be especially concerned by her celebration at the end of the dream. To celebrate something so dissonant speaks to the degree to which this pattern is embedded in her life. Even more revealing is the fact that she takes joy in the iteration and replication of this maladaptive behavior.

Alerted by the dream's presentation of unrealistic investments, I examined other areas in Jean's life where this theme might be evidenced. I asked about her relationship to money and her thoughts on what the training program would require. Regarding money, I asked specifically how much she was paying for analysis. She explained that because she had been making very little money when she began analysis, the analyst offered her a reduced fee of thirty-five dollars per session. The client appreciated the reduced fee, especially since she would have been unable to pay the regular fee of seventy-five dollars. Also, when asked about the commitment she would have to make to the training program and its effect on her life, Jean responded that her life would really not change much at all and that she would still have plenty of time to pursue other interests. As a graduate of a similar program, I can attest to the fact that one's life will inevitably be turned upside down by the emotional and energetic rigors of this type of postgraduate training.

Both the issue of the analytic fee and Jean's thoughts about the training program are captured in the dream imagery of paying an unrealistically low price for the apartment. More importantly, we find through associations that she is both unprepared and unaware of the psychological costs that the training program and a meaningful life itself will demand. Her unpreparedness was evident in other areas of her life, including her relationships and her living situation—she still lived at home with her parents.

As we look at Jean's continued confusion about what things cost psychologically, we see the degree to which her behavior has become a pattern through continual iterations. Here we are speaking of a type of "chreodic pattern," which as described by Waddington and more recently by Sheldrake, are those processes responsible (in part) for the development of memory and habituation within individuals and systems.

The first time a rainstorm pours down a mountain side looking for an outlet, it will create a suitable pathway down the hill. Gravity and other forces are important influences in the direction this pathway takes. However, with successive rainstorms, the system develops a memory of its previous trajectory. The original route, having become more fully delineated through successive iterations, evolves into a highly defined memory and pathway. A pattern is established. Similar mechanisms are at work in the replication of behavior in humans. While the idea of the chreode is helpful in understanding these dynamics, it is also somewhat limiting since it tends to describe causative processes. These informational fields are not created by any one trauma or through specific events in childhood. Rather, the archetype, like many laws, or habits, of nature, appears to have an *a priori* existence. However, temporal events may serve as immediate triggers for one's immersion into a particular field.

Jean's request and the therapist's acquiescence in the low fee served as the vehicle through which a particular pattern was repeated in the therapeutic situation. The therapist's acceptance of the low fee reflected his conscious effort to be sensitive to the client's financial reality. Yet I believe the dream indicates that the extent to which the low fee remained unanalyzed in the therapy served to alienate the patient further from a vital archetypal life task. Where the analysis should have helped her grasp the theme of psychological investment, instead she remained infantilized. This conclusion is also supported by the fact that the dream occurred during the fourth year of analysis, a substantial enough time period within which to have addressed this issue and to have made greater therapeutic progress than was evidenced. Of particular interest is the fact that after this interview, I had occasion to interview another candidate in treatment with this same analyst. Interestingly enough, the very same issues of money and infantilization appeared. Both clients remained, even during the later stages of the analysis, emotionally and archetypally unprepared for life. This confluence of issues suggests that the therapist was a more than willing participant in these dramas.

Such replicative dynamics are most often operative and enacted in the initial phase of treatment, where the treatment conditions are presented and, at times, negotiated. Here the client's request or acceptance of substantial alterations in the therapeutic frame served a purposive end, fueling the continuance of this life drama. The point here is not simply to view these client-therapist configurations as problematic, but to see them instead as highly choreographed, entrained dramas, serving as external mappings of internal, archetypal states.

In Jean's case, asking for and receiving the low fee represented a reenactment of her internal confusion about the commitments and psychological costs involved in undertaking life tasks. While it may have been possible analytically to address these concerns, the dream, as well as Jean's attitude about the training program, reflected the degree to which they had not been considered. The therapist, by being pulled unconsciously into the replicative process and not interpreting or rectifying the situation, most likely failed to help his client understand the archetypal issues of expense, commitment, and investment in the world.

The image of the landlord offering Jean a very low rent, like the therapist offering and never altering the low fee, indicates that the patient lived in the field of the missing father. Archetypally, the father offers the son or daughter a realistic understanding of the outer world, including information about the rites of passage needed to traverse the terrain from childhood to adulthood. What this candidate/ client needed was an understanding of the lingering emotional and outer world effects of the missing father and to shift to a more generative and related experience of the archetypal world of the father. In the course of the interview, the candidate revealed that she had in fact lost her father when she was very young. In an interesting and meaningful way, the admissions committee was being called on to respond to these archetypal dynamics and needs so as to provide the candidate with what the archetypal father would have offered. As we explained our reasons for not admitting her into the program at that time, I believe Jean understood on some level the significance of our interventions.

The Function and Manifestation of the Repetition in Treatment and Life

When the patient makes the initial phone call to inquire about beginning treatment, both patient and therapist bring to the encounter their own life histories, archetypal constellations, and fields. As the therapeutic field draws both patient and therapist into a new edition of a repetition, we can understand these recreations as incarnations and symbolizations of psyche in matter and of an underlying archetypal field. Jung addressed this point when he explained that we can never know the archetype directly but only through its symbolization.

We find the incarnation of archetypes in matter through the psyche's propensity to produce dreams rich in symbolic material, in fantasies and obsessions, and through the repetition compulsion. In this light, the dynamics that unfold between patient and therapist also can be seen as a representation of an archetypal pattern. This view of incarnation strengthens the idea of an autonomous, self-organizing dimension to the psyche.

The initiation of treatment serves to activate the dominant archetypal constellation within both members of the therapeutic dyad. The core complex embedded within the archetype tends to draw to it, like a magnetic field, self-similar/complex-similar interactions and information from the environment. For instance, the individual embedded in a submissive field will attract experiences from friends, colleagues, and associates that reflect the issues associated with this field. We begin to see the attracting power of the constellated archetypal field. While experiences of interactional repetitions are common both in treatment and in life, they are often reductively explained as the workings of a regressive, non-generative compulsion to repeat.

On one level, this reductive explanation is understandable and even partially correct. Consider for a moment how an individual deals with highly traumatic events occurring during childhood. Lacking the emotional and psychological resources to manage the trauma, a set of autonomic responses is established through which the individual emotionally closes off to the outside world, yet is unconsciously driven to repeat and relive the trauma. Much of the current work on Post Traumatic Stress Disorder validates this perspective. As Robert Langs suggests, the memory and effect of trauma is indeed recognized by the unconscious and functions as a vital agent and shaper of experiences within the individual psyche. The unconscious recognition and lasting effect of the trauma will never fade, even when effectively worked with in treatment.

What tends to occur under these conditions is the creation of an alignment to a particular field, like the incest or violence field. As treatment begins, the field often directs the types of interactions that take place between patient and therapist. While triggered by personal trauma, the field finds its matrix within an archetypal domain, which works to influence and dominate much of the individual's life.

In the presence of a weak ego structure, the influence of the archetypal field becomes stronger than the ego and begins to function virtually autonomously. Under these conditions, the strength of the archetypal field and its overwhelming control over the individual's life is similar to the autonomous functioning of the instincts. Archetypes, like instincts, serve as highly efficient agents for storing essential knowledge about life. While in no way hoping to glorify situations when archetypal functioning takes over ego consciousness, I wish to demonstrate that, in often uncanny ways, archetypal dominance, if understood and integrated by the ego, can become a valuable process.

As the archetype assumes increasing dominance over the ego, it creates situations and interactional patterns that can be viewed as the physical manifestations of the archetype. For instance, a child from a violent home will often find ways either to cultivate a violent response from others or, correspondingly, to elicit pity. Usually after the outbreak of yet another edition of this problem, the individual turns a perplexed face to the world and asks: "Why are these things happening to me?" To some extent, the individual participates in bringing about his own struggles. However, it may be far more accurate to see these behaviors as the functioning of an archetype that has taken over individual consciousness.

The power of fields and their ability to influence us have been examined from a number of perspectives, both in psychology and the sciences. Many references to this research have already been cited. One of the most important contributions to field theory comes from Ervin Laszlo, who explains that fields exist before the emergence of form. This is especially clear when we look at biological evolution and realize that the form a species eventually assumes is already present and functioning even before conception. Here perhaps we speak of an archetypal entelechy. Form and order emerge from these preformed, or form *in potentia*, fields. And, it is just a short leap to see how Laszlo's ideas regarding the generation of form and order, as well as the role of fields in creating these influences, seem to echo Jung's concept of archetypes.

Jung's theory of archetypes provides an important description of a nonmaterial, non-localized informational field theory. The Einstein-Podolsky-Rosen (EPR) experiments are also a fascinating study of non-local informational fields. In describing the impact of the EPR experiments, Heinz Pagels writes that:

> What the EPR argument did without making any assumptions about determinism or indeterminism was to show that quantum theory violated local causality. (*The World of Physics*, 472).

Adding to Pagels' description, David Bohm and Basil Hiley (1975) make the following comments about the EPR experiments:

> It is generally acknowledged that the quantum theory has many strikingly novel features, including discreetness of energy and momentum, discrete jumps in

quantum processes, wave particle duality, barrier penetration, etc. However, there has been too little emphasis on what is in our view, the most fundamentally different new feature of all, i.e., the intimate interconnection of different systems that are not in spatial contact. This has been especially clearly revealed through the . . . well known experiment of Einstein, Podolsky and Rosen. ("On the Intuitive Understanding of Non-Locality," (93-109)

Through perceptions like these, we can appreciate the existence and workings of fields and their power to create entrainment patterns. The acknowledgment that fields influence how we interact and behave in the world is growing. While it is essential to have a relatively stable personality structure and to engage with life in a conscious, deliberate manner, there are also times when we experience the stirrings of other, non-personally derived influences. Artists and athletes speak of being "in the zone." These are moments of pure grace, when the transpersonal enters and directs our lives and we feel part of a seamless whole. At these times, our behaviors and actions are influenced by the workings of archetypal fields.

The therapeutic frame, along with the therapeutic relationship itself, often becomes a paradigm of health in that it conveys to the patient that despite his/her fears and anxieties over conscious and unconscious forces, the clinician's stability and offer of a therapeutically sound environment will provide an alternate ego structure within which his or her anxieties can be metabolized. In addition to Langs' prolific writings on this theme, Peter Giovacchini (1984) echoes the importance of the therapeutic setting for the patient's health in the following:

Every analyst recognizes the unique features of the analytic frame of reference; what has not been sufficiently emphasized is that the setting itself helps the patient to consolidate his ego boundaries and to see himself as a separate, discrete individual. (*Character Disorders and Adaptive Mechanisms*, 373).

Later in this book, as an example of a larger phenomenon, I will explain how the conditions of treatment function as a stable attractor, drawing a powerful charge from both members of a therapeutic dyad.

Consider the dynamics operating in the field between patient and therapist in the following clinical vignette. The client, a twenty-seven-year-old male, left a message on my answering machine inquiring about therapy and asking me to return his call. When I reached him later in the day, I found his thoughts and speech pattern to be quite disjointed and fragmented, suggesting a great deal of distress and poor ego formation. During our brief conversation, he asked if I did any form of crystal therapy or trance work because, as he explained, he hoped to eliminate a series of troubling fantasies that had been disrupting his life and sleep for a number of months.

As he described his fears about these fantasies, I found myself interacting in an unconventional manner. Usually, I ask if the prospective client would like to set up a consultation to discourage any extended discussions of his or her concerns on the phone. This is done to alert the patient to the need to create a therapeutic environment with a relatively firm and stable set of parameters within which we can do our work. Especially when working with patients like this young man, whose thoughts were confused and who could not contain his anxieties, the offer of a therapeutically sound environment carries with it the promise of a healthy introjective experience that can eventually be borrowed from the therapist and, in time, imported and assimilated into the client's own personality.

However, for a variety of reasons, some more conscious than others, I responded to a number of the client's requests for information, answering his questions about my involvement in trance work, etc. and explaining that I did not do this type of therapy. Instead, I suggested that since his fantasies were causing distress, he might consider having a consultation. He agreed, but when I asked for his full name to write in my appointment book, my speech became a bit mumbled. In response to my garbled request, he answered not with his name, but with his phone number. Quickly he realized that I must already have that information since I had just called him, and so he asked me to repeat the question.

My behavior was uncharacteristic of how I generally handle a request for an initial interview. It is especially striking in light of the fact that my diploma thesis for the Jung Institute was about my study of "The Unconscious Dynamics of the Initial Interview" (1984).

In previous years, I would have focused solely on my own unconscious dynamics that resulted in my clumsy handling of the phone call and felt both clinically incompetent and ashamed. While I am still concerned about these unconscious dynamics, as my interests and experiences of archetypal fields have grown, I am now equally intrigued by the interactional dramas that emerge. I am suggesting that there are times when, in the interest of self-organization, the psyche will incarnate a certain set of dynamics between client and therapist, the meaning of which may remain unknown and mysterious for some time and may only be fully understood in retrospect. I realize, however, that discussing field-generated influences in treatment places us on thin ice in that one can simply say "The field made me do it" or that "It was the will of the archetypes." For instance, a handful of therapists and analysts have publicly stated that there are times when the Self demands sexual involvement between client and therapist. While I have clear evidence of the power of fields to structure interactional dynamics, any therapist that could ever believe that the Self sanctions sexual involvement with a client is bordering on psychotic inflation. So, while we need to allow for non-ego influences in interactions, we must still evaluate their possible meaning without having to enact their dynamics.

An illustration of this point is found in the following clinical vignette that I heard in a supervisory seminar. Jane, a prospective client, called for an initial appointment with a therapist named Julia. In giving directions, Julia explained that her office was located at 341 Providence Street, next to a flower shop called "Remembrance." At the appointed time for the session, Jane had not yet arrived. She soon called, explaining to the therapist that she could find no office at

341 Providence. The therapist suddenly realized that she had given her the wrong address—341 instead of 841 Providence—and quickly corrected her mistake.

At this point, I asked the therapist to stop for a moment while I made a number of comments. In realizing the degree of fidelity between the unfolding of events in the client/ therapist relationship and those in the respective lives of each party, I suspected that the therapeutic enterprise was already embedded in a field of abandonment. I speculated that since the therapeutic relationship had already experienced such a striking beginning and constellated specific issues about abandonment and being forgotten (especially noteworthy is the store's name "Remembrance"), the client had in all probability experienced a severe break in her earliest attachment to her mother and was quite likely an orphan. I added that the behavior of the therapist suggested that she also had an equally strong connection to the field of abandonment and loss. The therapist confirmed my reading of the events, explaining that the client was in fact an orphan. And, in the therapist's life, there also had been a recent, profound loss.

In studying the initial interview in clinical practice for more than fifteen years, I have come to see that the events which evolve within the client-therapist field often represent a mapping of the internal processes of both parties. Even the minute details of the therapeutic contact or, as we saw in this case, the more dramatic unfolding of events stand as part of a larger, overarching field. Singular events can be viewed as holographic encapsulations of the entire field. The larger field can be read in reverse—its nature can be inferred by the constellation of events occurring around it. Each detail is informationally rich and descriptive of the field. As described later in this book, an individual is often oriented toward a particular archetypal alignment, a stable attractor site, working in much the same manner as a complex to organize his or her behavior in correspondence with the central dynamics of the constellated complex/attractor.

The bi-personal nature of the clinical enterprise, with its emphasis on replicative dynamics, along with the opportunity to metabolize archetypal contents, presents an occasion for both client and therapist to evolve. This idea parallels Jung's concept of the "marriage quaternity" in that both the client and therapist's conscious and unconscious dynamics are activated and influenced during treatment. If the therapy is to succeed, both members will experience some degree of psychological growth. While the idea of a patient/therapist interactive field is acknowledged among therapists, rarely is it afforded its due weight in creating the dynamics that evolve in therapy. These dynamics are as much archetypally derived as they are personally.

I am suggesting an archetypally driven, developmental theory of self-organization for processes occurring within the natural world, the human psyche, and the therapeutic relationship. While archetypal pattern recognition may afford us a glimpse into one's fate, the proposed evolution of the human psyche is more often understood retrospectively. James Hillman thoughtfully addresses this point in his book *The Soul's Code,* where he suggests that a certain destiny factor is operative and visible even in the earliest movements and influences in an individual's life. Jung also makes this point in the following:

> [T] he symbols of wholeness frequently occur at the beginning of the individuation process, indeed they can often be observed in the first dreams of early infancy. This observation says much for the *a priori* existence of potential wholeness, and on this account the idea of *entelechy* instantly recommends itself . . . . [*I*]*t looks as if something already existent were being put together* (*CW 9i,* § 278, italics mine)

One may be able to piece together the order operating within the psyche after a particular situation or change has occurred. An example of this sense of a preformed order, or goal, can be more easily understood in the following story. I remember driving home from an analytic session and listening to the radio when a tape of a women singing on the Ted Mack Amateur Hour Show, popular back in the 50s and 60s, was played. It was one of the most beautiful, resonant, mature voices I had ever heard. The announcer then explained that the tape was of Judy Garland's debut on television, when she was less than ten years old. I wondered how such a beautiful and mature voice could be housed in the body of a child. Similar to Hillman's discussion of Judy Garland in *The Soul's Code*, I suddenly had a glimpse into the challenges she had to endure and perhaps could even begin to understand why she had such a troubled and tragic life. Her God-given abilities were almost too great for a child to contain. The voice was otherworldly, but she had to live in the space-time world of childhood and was never able to successfully traverse the bridge between these two worlds.

While we may choose to believe that the direction one's life takes is predominately a matter of personal freedom, it is prudent to give the Self its due as the primary mover of human experience. To a large extent, life is influenced by *la forza del destino* ("the force of destiny"). Jung's work supports a belief in the hidden operations of the psyche that strive to achieve a goal unknown to the individual personality. Jung writes:

> It is to be hoped that experiences in the years to come will sink deeper shafts into this obscure territory, on which I have been able to shed but a fleeting light, and will discover more about the secret workshop of the daemon who shapes our fate. (*CW 9i*, § 278)

Here we can see that the goal of Jung's psychology involves a mature recognition of one's own archetypal morphology and destiny and the development of a personal and differentiated response to it. The model of the individual working with the transpersonal is echoed in many theologies, which address our need to know deity and to work in cooperation with it. So too do I draw on the advice of my colleague and friend Richard Ott, who reminded me that the difference between destiny and fate is character, which suggests the need to establish a personal relationship to these transpersonal, archetypal forces.

This point was highlighted a number of years ago in a supervisory session I had with Yoram Kaufmann. Discussing a particular case, I presented my client's dream:

> Close to ten cords of cherry wood were piled up, log length (each tree about twenty to thirty feet long) in a field. It appeared that it was left to age to increase its value as firewood.

Realizing the value of cherry wood in fine woodworking and in making furniture, I understood that to use it for firewood suggested that something of real value, either an attitude or a talent, was not being utilized to its full potential by my client. In discussing this dream and my sense of alarm for the client, the analysis, and my own psyche,[1] Kaufmann drew my attention to one central feature of the dream that I had overlooked—the fact that the wood was only being *considered* for firewood. He explained that the fact that the wood still lay in the field meant that there was a question as to how this valuable wood / psychological / archetypal attitude would be utilized and metabolized by the client and analyst.

My initial mistake in handling this material was to see the imagery as suggesting that the client and therapist *had already misused* something of great value. However, the actual details of the dream suggested instead that something of great value was still present, but that it could easily be used in such a way as to not bring out its inherent value and beauty.

This experience reinforced the need to be vigilant and disciplined when working with symbolic material. However, the specificity of the image still alerts us to the underlying morphology of the psychological situation—namely, the need to find a way of life commensurate with one's intrinsic nature.

In realizing that much of life is lived both in response to and under the influence of archetypal fields, it is easy to perceive that these same operations are at work within human relationships. As archetypal incarnation and representation is achieved and eventually

---

1. Dreams often say as much about the therapist's psyche as they do about the patient's. This is because dreams occur within a therapeutic relationship, are embedded within a bi-personal field, and are subject to all the previously mentioned processes such as entrainment, coherency, and synchronization.

responded to, we begin to see that an important dimension of the repetition requires conversion of archetypal material and information contained within the field into usable psychological form whereby we can discover its meaning.

Once the archetypal imperative is understood, it can then find a corresponding expression in the individual's life and work. In this manner, we have the conversion of archetypal, symbolic material into matter, enabling the energetic core of the archetype and its information to become accessible to the personality. On the other hand, when these processes remain unconscious and repetition occurs without understanding, a pattern is established for an endless cycle of repetitive, non-generative activity. At this point, the system, be it the human personality or a system in the natural world, functionally closes off to new information, spinning farther in the direction of circularity and meaninglessness.

Jung comments on the need to wrestle a personal life from these natural, vegetative processes in the following:

> When nature is left to herself, energy is transformed along the lines of its natural "gradient." In this way natural phenomena are produced, but not "work." So also man when left to himself lives as a natural phenomenon, and, in the proper meaning of the word, produces no work. It is culture that provides the machine whereby the natural gradient is exploited for the performance of work. (*CW 8*, § 80)

While essential for certain developmental needs, the tendency toward pattern repetition exists as a product of nature and not of human design. I have come to view repetition as nature's way of preserving form and insuring that each new iteration of a particular design remains consistent with its underlying morphology. However, the work of understanding the core of the archetype, as suggested by Jung, is what drives personal evolution past the autopoietic dimension of the repetition compulsion and toward greater differentiation and complexity. Diversification, which in many ways is an evolutionary advance from the replicative order, is introduced later in the life process, perhaps in the same way that a conscious working through of an archetypal repetition is often only possible as a secondary process. We may never be able to know the origins of those forces responsible for the unfolding and developing of life. However, we can infer the nature of a constellated archetype through its emergence in patterns.

CHAPTER SIX

The Emergence of Matter from Psyche
The Generation of Form from Pattern Repetition

As seen from the Zukav material quoted earlier and from many discoveries in particle physics, we now understand that whenever two entities—whether particles, animals, or individuals—enter a field, there will inevitably be some type of interaction. The two most common trajectories for these interactions are attraction and repulsion.

As we borrow the lens of modern physics and apply its findings to the therapeutic relationship, we create an interesting and potentially more useful way to understand the power of recreation and the generation of form that occur between client and therapist. The time is ripe to move past our conventional closed systems and unidirectional view of interchange that, through our reliance on both traditional and revised perspectives on transference and countertransference, draw us ultimately into a reductively driven dead end. Instead, our perspectives on interactional dynamics need to catch up with the important discoveries in the new sciences, which alert us to the more profound, dynamic, and interconnected nature of relationships. The researcher Eric Kandel found that even engaging in a conversation produced important changes in the neuronal wiring of each individual. Given such findings, isn't it time to shift our paradigm even further? Underlying, archetypal influences are responsible for the variations in form found not only in the therapeutic relationship, but also in all relationships.

FIELD, FORM, AND FATE

Clinical Presentation

A therapeutic example of the generation of form that can be observed in the initial encounter involves a forty-five-year-old woman who called and left a message on my answering machine, hoping to set up an appointment. In the phone message, she explained in a somewhat breathy delivery that she needed help. While the details of her phone message appeared sincere, I was left with the impression of having heard a finely studied presentation. Also, since she spoke rather rapidly, I was unable to discern her last name. When I returned her call, I introduced myself and asked if she was "Mary." I prefer to have a client's last name, because addressing someone I do not know by his or her first name suggests a familiarity inconsistent with the inception of the therapeutic situation.

She thanked me for returning her call and repeated that she needed to talk to someone. She thought that a Jungian analyst could understand her situation. Mary then explained that, if she were to see me for a consultation, she would need a number of questions answered on the phone prior to the session. I asked if she could wait until the interview to have this discussion, but she quickly replied that in order to feel secure enough to make the appointment, she wanted more information about me. She then asked where I had trained. I hesitated, because I find that to respond to manifest, surface-oriented questions often impedes the communication of deep unconscious material. However, contrary to what I had hoped to do, I explained that I was a Jungian Analyst, trained at the Jung Institute in New York. Once I opened the door to this professional/self disclosure, she proceeded to ask about my clinical perspectives and then quickly added to this list of questions, "How old are you?"

After more than twenty-five years of studying the nature of the initial interview, I have consistently found that virtually every form of self-disclosure by the therapist leads to an unending series of manifest communications from the client, thus risking the loss of contact with derivative, unconscious communications. While I had reluctantly responded to her initial questions, I explained that I thought it was in

98

the best interest of the prospective treatment if I did not say any more about myself. Mary then responded: "I don't think this treatment will work for me if you already have this attitude."

When a client begins asking personal questions and is unable to tolerate the frustration of not having many of these questions answered, it often points to a poor prognosis because it indicates that he or she is embedded in a highly replicative, enclosed system. In these instances, the client will only accept the therapist if he or she accedes and conforms to the client's internal dynamics. To vary most often results in an early termination. Any system that is governed by such a tight and strict replicative order suggests a fundamentalist's approach to life, thus giving evidence of a fragile identity. The more creative and expansive the ego, the more it desires and is able to engage in new experiences, whereas a more fragile system defends itself against anything new, because it perceives the new as threatening. In viewing the treatment environment as an externalization of the internal dynamics existing between the client and clinician, the analytic task is to assess how these internal dynamics tend to be evacuated and externalized. I have called this type of patient-therapist interaction an "externalization of internal manic defense processes." In part, this idea builds on the work presented in D. W. Winnicott's paper entitled "The Manic Defense." In these cases, internal dread, fears, and terrors, along with their corresponding defenses, become reenacted and reactivated in the treatment, often with the therapist's interventions operating in tandem with the client's manic defensives.

In this case, both clinician and prospective client were responding to a series of perturbations in the initial phone interaction. An interactional pattern was set in motion where both members of the therapeutic dyad behaved in response to a series of prompts, which were archetypally derived. Here I am suggesting an interactional pattern informed as much by a set of morphogenetic constraints as by the personal dynamics of each member of the dyad.

An hour after this conversation, I checked my answering machine to find that Mary had called again saying that she was disturbed by our previous conversation and would like to talk further with me about the prospect of beginning treatment. In her next call, Mary described her discomfort with our conversation, confessing serious doubts about being able to work with me. She went on to say that, unless she had more information about me, she could not justify being vulnerable to the analytic process and to me. She then added what I feel was probably the most telling piece of information about her psyche and the nature of the rapport we had already established. She said that it would be "mutually beneficial" if I would just agree to answer her questions, since she would then feel better about me and, in turn, I would collect my consultation fee.

This was the last straw for me, since the comment about a mutually beneficial situation spoke to a type of psychopathy of which I wanted no part. I responded by saying that if I were to do anything to encourage or entice her into coming for the session, I would be acting immorally and unethically. I added that I did not want to get involved in any more phone interactions. If she wanted an interview, I would see her and discuss her concerns at that time.

However much I might prefer to see Mary's psychopathy as belonging only to her psyche, I have to admit that her comment, which suggested the existence of a destructive alignment, spoke pointedly to the type of relationship in which I had already agreed to participate with her. Since I had already answered her initial questions, she had every reason to view me as yet another unethical, seductive, and manipulative man. While there may be a number of perspectives from which I could justify my initial phone behavior, there still exists a level of manipulation that has to be addressed. Yet, as the following material will explain, I preferred to continue investigating the nature and specificity of the interactional dynamics emerging in the therapeutic relationship, rather than simply attribute them to mutual neurotic complexes.

Surprisingly, after my rebuff of her bargain, Mary suddenly asked if we could schedule a consultation, ending the conversation by saying that she would have to think about whether she could keep the appointment and that she would call and let me know her decision. The next morning she called to say that she would keep the appointment and see me later that day. When it was time for the appointment, I went to the waiting area. Mary greeted me with a sarcastic, "Hello, so you must be Michael." I knew I was caught in a complex when I felt subtly annoyed and observed the tone of my voice when I responded, "Hello, Mary, yes, I'm Dr. Conforti." The patient responded tartly: "Well, if you are Dr. Conforti, then I'm Dr. Smith, since I have a doctorate in business administration." She went on to repeat that she did not think this treatment would work. I said that maybe it would not, but suggested that we go into the office and talk.

After a few brief words of introduction about herself and her situation, Mary looked at me and asked: "Now could you tell me a little about yourself?" While I had anticipated as much from her, I had hoped that the last phone call had daunted her need to solicit personal information from me. When I suggested that she just try to say whatever came to her mind, Mary let me know how much she resented my intervention. Then, she reluctantly told me about her prior experiences in treatment. She explained that the last time she had considered entering therapy, she had interviewed a number of therapists. Two of them also viewed the initial session as clinically important and had similarly declined to divulge personal information about themselves. Additionally, these therapists had charged a fee for the first appointment (as I did), which had annoyed her. However, the third prospective clinician told her that the first session was a time for both of them to get to know one another and, since it was a sort of "get together," there certainly would be no fee. "Do you know," she asked me, "whom I chose?" As if one needed to intuit the answer, she proudly announced that "It was the one who didn't charge me."

The unpaid interview and the informality of her chosen clinician were consistent with the pattern she had already displayed in our conversations and, to a degree, were also descriptive of my solicitous behavior toward her. This type of therapeutic exchange and environment offers the client the opportunity to gain mastery over the clinician in that informality all too often speaks to a high degree of seductiveness within a clinician's psyche. In this type of coupling, whatever unconscious dynamics the client is living with will be further sequestered from consciousness because the therapist has adopted a relational style consistent with his own personal need to defend against important aspects of his psyche. I am not suggesting that every therapist who answers a client's questions is behaving in a non-therapeutic manner, but that such behavior often speaks to an overall pattern in which seduction, manipulation, and denial serve as important cornerstones in his or her psychological makeup.

Mary continued the session with me, saying "I really don't like your type of interview, and I think you really should tell me something about yourself." Here I made a brief intervention, which was quite uncharacteristic of me, and explained that I thought we were caught in a difficult impasse; she wanted me to continue talking about myself, as I had done in the initial phone call, and I strongly felt it would be unhealthy to do so. I added that to continue in this manner would serve to seal off other more important aspects of what she might need to discuss, such as her daughter's drug problems and the numerous infidelities in her marriage. I again suggested that she just say whatever came to mind, basically re-explaining the idea of free association.

It is important to add that while I had an idea as to the possible reason for my defensiveness, it was premature of me to address these provocative, interactional dynamics. Grudgingly, Mary conceded. She began telling an interesting story filled with meaning. She explained that she had been married for twenty years and that a number of years ago she had begun an affair with another man. The affair went on for some time without her husband ever finding out. Then she realized that she had "just stopped growing" with her spouse and wanted out of the marriage.

She was now staying in the area temporarily, waiting for her lover to arrive. Together they would decide where to settle down. However, because the lover was still involved in his own complicated and unresolved marriage, he was having second thoughts about join-ing her. Mary was quite depressed about this turn of events. She then added that her daughter had been in and out of trouble since her youth and was now roaming aimlessly on the West Coast.

In discussing her professional life, Mary explained that she helped start up new businesses in underdeveloped communities around the country. Through her efforts many people had gained a sense of confidence and pride in themselves and their work; many of them now possessed a new sense of independence.

At this point, I intervened, explaining that it was striking that after I had mentioned our impasse and suggested that she free associ-ate, rather than continue asking me to disclose personal information about myself, she suddenly recalled situations in which she had felt both satisfaction and unrest. I then said that her own unfaithfulness in her marriage may have been similar to how I behaved in our initial phone call in that by responding to her request for personal informa-tion and proceeding to offer her a limited number of details, I had essentially deceived her by not maintaining a reflective, inquisitive, and thoughtful position. She might have even perceived me as being lost like her daughter, in that my behavior had been somewhat manipulative, carried out in the hope of filling the hour. However, when I had elucidated our impasse, she allowed herself to speak freely of situations in which she had helped people and of the tremendous contributions she was now making to needy communities. Perhaps, I added, those stories reflected her feelings about me and what treat-ment was and could be if we shifted out of our defensive style, laced with the demand for control and power. I added that it seemed to me that her feelings and fear of experiencing security were con-nected to regrets and losses, such as those she spoke about in relation to her daughter and to her marriage.

There was a noticeable shift in the field between us during Mary's free associations and immediately after my interpretation. Her initial recalcitrance and my resentments toward her had abated. However, as we approached the end of the session, Mary closed with the following: "I still don't know what you have to offer me in the treatment." She suggested: "Why don't you give me a call, if you think you can help me, and let me know what you think you can do for me?" With that, she paid for the interview and left.

Analysis of the Session

Communication is provocative. It disseminates information, reveals the underlying archetypal field of the communicator, and creates a field of influence between the speaker and the listener. Such a field was in evidence in the beginning stages of our communications. My ideas on the workings of archetypal fields suggest that as each communication emerges from a relatively stable underlying archetypal constellation, the resultant interactions within the system involve a recreation and incarnation of an archetypal morphology. While there are many attendant dangers in this sort of enactment and the ensuing coupling processes, they are nevertheless natural occurrences. Recall that emergence is nature's way of communication. As Portmann helps us see in the bird's plumage and song a communication about its life, so too do we find, in these fascinating interactional configurations, the psyche expressing itself to anyone interested in listening.

The interactive dynamics emerging between us stirred a strong degree of skepticism and agitation in me. Already at an early stage of contact, we find the presence of a perturbation effecting the movement of the therapeutic system. One has to continually ask if the perturbation works to create an entrainment with the original replicative dynamics and, if so, could it foster new growth and movement? However, repeated experiences in these initial interviews reveal a movement toward iterations of the original dynamics that, if not interpreted and changed, will result in a poor prognosis.

In order for a system to evolve from simple replication toward greater complexity, it must reach a position far from equilibrium, termed a third state system. Writing on perturbations and their role in moving a system to a third state field, Richard Jensen (1987), a Yale physicist, writes: " . . . the perturbation must become rather large before the evolution of a single phase trajectory begins . . ." ("Classical Chaos," 174)

A serious perturbation occurred during our first phone conversation when Mary asked about my personal and professional background. While her questions may appear innocuous and ones to be expected in the initial interview, I have found that this particular communicative style often reveals disturbances in the client's psyche. The persistence of such questions and the client's insistence that I answer suggest an inability to contain anxiety and flight into a manic-defensive position. Also, because there was so little freedom permitted within this interactional exchange, one can intuit the presence of a stable/fixed attractor site working to constrain the parameters of the relationship.

One may question why I prefer to discuss these dynamics in terms of field theory, rather than simply describing the client's behavior as learned, defensive, replicative, and originating solely out of her personal experiences and dynamics. To proceed with these limited formulations throws us back into a mechanistic logjam. The notion of an open system, working to create dissipative structures, greater complexity, and higher degrees of freedom, speaks more accurately to what I have seen occurring in the therapeutic situation. When we say that the client is utilizing whatever defenses she can to protect herself, we see her behavior reductively, as highly disturbed and pathological, rather than purposive and serving to choreograph a structured, and perhaps teleological, drama. Clearly, the maintenance of defenses is vital to the life of any system, but there is more at work than simply survival.

However, to follow the implications and threads of these proposed paradigm shifts, we also have to revisit the idea of defenses. As we shift the model from pathology to one of expression, we find that virtually everything the system does is a way of expressing its unique identity. Defenses are nature's way of providing for self-protection and are part and parcel of the innate organization of life on every level. They are non-pathological expressions of self. If we alter our paradigm, we can view these early disturbances as the system's attempt to provide an external mapping of its internal, archetypal morphology. Once this archetypal blueprint is understood, the treatment relationship then has the opportunity to go from replication to greater degrees of freedom. In doing so, the client can move from a singular alignment to one facet of an archetype to a broader range of archetypal alignments and possibilities.

As a system or an individual continues to spin within a repetitive mode, the parameters are increasingly narrowed, thus limiting the opportunity for growth. However, in order for a system to maintain fidelity to its original design, in its initial stages of development it must remain refractory to new inputs of information and energy. A major function of replication is to maintain and subsidize the system's primary design and ontology. Repetition virtually ensures the continuance of a regime, but it does not necessarily create the prompts for new life and diversity.

The dynamics manifested in Mary's initial phone call were in many respects different from the conscious intention of either participant. Instead, they evolved in response to a series of underlying processes, mandates, and tendencies inherent in both the archetypal configuration of the therapeutic relationship and between the members of the dyad.[1]

Mary's interactional style was controlling. We can say that, for many personal and archetypal reasons, she was embedded in a field dominated by control and fear. As the field exerts its influence in much the same manner as a magnet configures iron fillings, it draws virtually everything into its orbit, including others.

There are many creative and interesting applications of this theme of influencing fields. One involves studies of twins separated at birth. The findings are that, in many cases, twins' respective lives parallel one another in unlikely ways—they may have the same taste in clothes, give their children the same names, marry spouses with the same name, etc.

---

1. It bears repeating that similar evolution occurs in all archetypally fueled relationships; that is, all relationships in the natural world.

THE EMERGENCE OF MATTER FROM PSYCHE

In physics, the Einstein-Podolsky-Rosen experiments of 1935 also speak to the issue of interconnectivity.

> Two distinct electrons are correlated in a non-local way. This is because their correlation is an expression of an underlying symmetry principle. They are a-causally connected. They form an undivided whole. (F. David Peat, personal communication)

Like many others, I interpret the results of the EPR experiments as further validation of the non-local transmission of information. However, Beverly Rubik and F. David Peat explained to me that to discuss a transfer of information implies that we are talking about separate, distinct things. They both pointed out that the beauty of the EPR results is that they reveal the primacy of the underlying symmetry, coherence, and unity existing in the world. In this worldview, there is no need for one entity to send information and a separate entity to receive it, since interconnection already exists. And, as my findings in the therapeutic domain suggest, this underlying unity is in fact a more accurate rendering of the events that effect and relate individuals to one another. F. David Peat suggests that:

> There is a field connecting the two and the action of one A modifies or modulates the signal and this is transmitted as information, a message, influence to B. But to do this means that A and B are no longer an undivided whole. Or to put it another way, as soon as you try to disturb A, you break the correlation between A and B. Physicists have shown that any attempt to use the EPR correlations as a way to send signals from A and B will have the effect of destroying the correlation. (personal communication)

So instead of a transfer of information, we do well to shift the paradigm to one where a tuning and receptivity to interconnectivity accounts for many of the fascinating occurrences where two individuals access each other's highly private and personal thoughts.

Mary's controlling dynamics served to maintain a state of equilibrium within her psyche and in her interpersonal relationships.

The recursive nature of the repetition keeps the individual within a constricted, fixed, and familiar orbit. Here, we can see how the repetitive order maintains a functionally closed system and informational loop, as opposed to an open system that continually receives the input of new information from the environment. Csanyi and Kampis (1991), both leading researchers in the area of replicative theory, describe the relationship between replication and closed systems:

> In the identical replication stage the system is function-
> ally closed and its replication continues as long as the
> environment does not change. There are no further organi-
> zational changes initiated by organizational causes,
> because no new functions can originate. ("Modelling
> Biological and Social Change," 81)

They add that the " . . . system becomes an autonomous self-maintaining unity ... (which) produces exactly the same network which has originally produced it." (81-82)

The functionally closed nature of our interactive, repetitive dance indicated that I would only be accepted into Mary's world if I behaved in accordance with the rules of the particular, constellated field. If I had offered her what I thought would have been a more suitable first phone contact, there would have been absolutely no opportunity to have had our consultation, since she would have rejected me, most probably, off hand. I found myself behaving in a way that compromised my therapeutic values and confirmed Mary's unconscious perceptions and expectations about therapists as being destructive. Through my actions, Mary could further cauterize herself from her internal turmoil over her daughter's situation.

I must emphasize that the interactions that occurred between us were not fully driven by personal dynamics or consciously intended by either the client or therapist. On the contrary, the objective psyche's attempts to create resonance along these lines represent the operations of the field itself that created an interactional configuration congruent with its dominant, in which the patient and the therapist were embedded.

THE EMERGENCE OF MATTER FROM PSYCHE

All systems evolve to the point of converting potential into form through the creation of resonance patterns. Everything grows and evolves by establishing a relationship to something else. Without a foundation based in self-replicating, resonating patterns, a system's opportunity for development is seriously jeopardized.

This position posits that volition and individual will, while essential in life, often are relegated to a back seat in these processes and dynamics. Instead, archetypal, morphogenetic processes play a much larger role in structuring the emergence of form in the natural world and in human relationships, including the treatment situation.

CHAPTER SEVEN

From Form to Chaos to Higher Form

C haos theory and discoveries in the new sciences offer insights into the possible meaning of initial perturbations described in the last chapter. A number of books and articles published within the last five to ten years have made contributions to our understanding of these dynamics: I. Prigogine and I. Stengers' *Order Out of Chaos: Man's New Dialogue with Nature*, Ervin Laszlo's *Evolution: The Grand Synthesis* and *Evolution: The Cosmic Dimension*, Gary Zukav's *The Dancing Wu Li Masters*, Ivar Ekeland's *Mathematics and the Unexpected*, Vilmos Csanyi's *Evolutionary Systems and Society*, F. David Peat's *Synchronicity: The Bridge Between Matter and Mind*, David Bohm and David Peat's *Science, Order and Creativity: A Dramatic New Look at the Creative Roots of Science and Life*, and Christopher Alexander's *Pattern Language*. In developmental biology, I also find the work of Paul Rapp, Brian Goodwin, Peter Saunders, and Mae-Wan Ho invaluable.

My investigations into the role of initial perturbations in the therapeutic field led to a 1990 paper entitled "The Role of Chaotic Attractors in the Therapeutic System," which I wrote as part of a research team. This paper discussed how chaos functions within the therapeutic setting in much the same way as it does in the life process—by creating non-linearity and non-periodic phase transitions. However, there appears to be a dual trajectory and aim to the perturbations that appear in the therapeutic situation. The first runs contrary to our usual understanding of perturbation theory. Rather than propel the system into a novel and third state field, the perturbations first provoke and entrain the members of the therapeutic dyad into a pattern expressive of a constellated archetype. Unique configurational processes shape the relationship to fit the contours of a prearranged design and trajectory in much the same way that a stable attractor shapes and contains, constrains and designs a system—like a pendulum in a fixed limit cycle. Then, once the replicative regime is established and secured, the system is often brought to a bifurcation point through which novelty and complexity can enter. The eventual movement toward bifurcation reflects the natural tendency of the system and the psyche toward health and order. Despite the conservative nature of replicative phenomena, the psyche still pushes for new life and growth.

Built into the life of virtually every organism are ways to move it to greater levels of complexity. Through the appearance of challenges and perturbations to the prior level of organization, systems will have to either adapt to these changes or remain entrenched within a simple replicative regime. So too in the life of therapeutic relationships. While on one hand perturbations in therapy can be viewed as expressions of deviation, transference-countertransference mishaps, etc., they also present occasions where growth can take place.

In growing up on the streets of Brooklyn, we learned quickly that a Pollyanna approach to life would inevitably lead to trouble. So I assure the reader that my understanding of the role perturbations play in treatment is born out of experience, not illusion. Systems often go from utilizing replicative dynamics in their development to stages of non-periodic, non-replicative functioning. So enters the role of chaos and non-linearity. This helps us to understand why virtually every therapy either begins or evolves to a point where the very dynamics with which the patient internally struggles become embedded in the analytic relationship.

I discuss one of the more dramatic examples I have seen of a perturbation created through a repetition in a 1987 paper entitled "Child Analysis: A Patient's Response to Disruptions in the Frame," which illustrates the details of what led up to my final session with an eight-year-old girl. There were a number of difficulties, collusions, and perturbations involved from the beginning. To start, the child's mother got my name through one of my former students. Also, because of the financial situation of the mother, who was recently divorced with two small children and little income, I agreed to half my normal fee. An additional perturbation took place during the initial interview, when after meeting with the child for thirty-five minutes, I asked her to leave the room while I met briefly with her mother. This was clearly a mistake. I was quite insensitive to the dynamics of the child and the family, which were discussed in subsequent sessions. Also, prior to the final appointment, the patient's mother suddenly reneged on her initial agreement to pay for missed sessions and wanted me to discuss my treatment of the little girl with her schoolteacher. In addition, the mother asked me to change the appointment time. When the mother explained that she would not allow her daughter to continue treatment if her requests were not met, I agreed to them for a number of reasons that in time I had to carefully reconsider.

Because I felt so lost in this case, I decided to accept wholeheartedly my supervisor's recommendation that I respond only to the client's derivative communications. This means that I was to attend only to her unconscious communications and pass over all other manifest, consciously derived ones. While I felt that such a response would be too much for her to tolerate, my confusion about the case and conflicting feelings about how to handle the mother's requests strengthened my need to ignore my own leanings and accept my supervisor's suggestions. However, as the following material illustrates, even my interactions within supervision aligned with the nature of the drama enacted within this little girl's life.

In the last session the patient arrived visibly depressed. The following is a summation of the themes she presented:

> You know that there isn't any Santa Claus. I don't believe in him anymore ... My father just did something very strange with the house that he built. I even helped him build it. I cut and nailed some of the floorboards. It was something that we did together that was very important to me, and I

113

> thought to him. Suddenly he decided to sell it. Why is he giving away something we built together? I just can't understand this. I also watched this horror movie the other night while I was with Daddy in which all the men were vaporized.

These derivative images contain objectively valid perceptions about my acquiescing to the demands of the client's mother and accepting a set of supervisory suggestions that ran contrary to what I believed appropriate. I suggested to the patient that, as with the house she cared about so much and even helped build with her father, we too had worked together to build our therapeutic relationship. However, in agreeing to change a number of the conditions of therapy and deferring to my supervisor, I gave our therapeutic home away. I added that she might have felt that her father and now I were giving away something that was important to her, and that I too might be acting impulsively in strange and frightening ways. (While I internally acknowledged the supervisory issue and its role in our work, it was best not to comment on it to her). I added that since she was now aware of the loss of her father, of their house, and of her previously intact family, she might also be feeling a sense of loss about our work and the "house" we had built together. The men in her life—the father, the therapist, and the archetypal world of the protective father in general—had all been vaporized as in her dream.

The child never returned after this session. I was sad to lose the case. However, I learned a great deal about the repetition of patterns in treatment and about those unresolved issues from my own life that created the grounds out of which this entrainment ensued and which inevitably complicated therapy. The entrainment and replication were such that the girl experienced yet another male father figure unable to provide an ongoing sense of protection and stability. Through my responses to the mother and to my supervisor, the child's past and, to some degree, my own past had been recreated in our relationship. She had again lost her father.

The call for a replicative experience is also often seen in the case of incest patients where it is inevitable that some form of bound-

ary issue or concern will be generated within the treatment relationship. After a difficult session, for instance, the client may ask for an
additional appointment or if the therapist will treat a friend of his or
hers or a family member. In more extreme cases, the client may ask
the therapist for a hug or another form of physical contact, all of which
are especially provocative.

The client's requests, as well as the events occurring within the
therapeutic dyad which evoked them, represent a highly complicated
situation with serious implications for treatment. Often a client
unconsciously experiences the therapist's fulfillment of his or her
requests as seductive and as a tacit willingness to become involved in
a compromised treatment. This type of therapeutic experience casts
the client/therapist relationship into the incest field. If the therapist
grants the client's requests, he or she is often experienced as similar to the incest figure from the past. If the therapist works toward
understanding these dynamics, rather than moving toward enactment
of them, he or she also becomes an equally terrifying figure. The latter situation is provocative and potentially dangerous because, as the
therapist demonstrates his or her understanding of the incest pull, by
not capitulating to such demands and behaviors, he or she instead
becomes a model of security and trust. The client will unconsciously
realize that the clinician can manage and understand his or her needs
and internal difficulties and may be able to let down his or her
defenses. However, as defenses weaken, vulnerabilities increase, along
with a reactivation of memories of what happened earlier in life, when
he or she trusted someone.

On the other hand, there are times when the unconscious urge to
repeat will dominate the treatment. For instance, the patient may call
between sessions asking for some form of reassurance. While it is
advisable to suggest that the patient wait until the following session
to discuss his or her feelings and concerns, there are times when a
brief phone call is necessary. The response to the call and the accepted
invitation to communicate outside of the therapist's office will have
powerful implications for the treatment. However, there is a world of

difference between the offer to give a hug and a phone call. Because a hug involves physical contact, it may trigger a new edition of the earlier trauma, and there will certainly be a strong degree of material activated, if the clinician decides to hug the client. However, while also provocative, the phone call, albeit a boundary concern, merely resonates with the earlier incest trauma; it is an extension of boundaries, not a severe violation of them. In my experience, a close parallel to the initial trauma—like a hug—creates difficulties, whereas a phone call is a more workable perturbation.

While both events are perturbations, according to Richard Jensen's descriptions of strong and weak perturbations, the hug draws the therapist further into the realm of the original incest figure and incest field. This provocative type of response is most often too powerfully laden an event for either the patient or the therapist to metabolize and is usually experienced by the client as invasive. In my experience in supervising clinicians, I have found a strong correspondence between a therapist's willingness to engage in boundary violations and his or her own often traumatized past, which has remained unresolved, even over the course of extended treatment.

Having provided some clinical examples of the repetition of patterns, I would now like to return to the issue of the function of the repetition. Remember that in the paradigm I am presenting, the repetition stands as an autonomous event, morphogenetically coded, with an informationally rich set of directives that regulate its developmental trajectory. Nature and the Self create these habits and tendencies, not the patient or therapist.

The original traumatic event, or series of events, will find its way into the treatment, most often through the repetition of a set of experiences similar to the formative situation. It appears that such repetitions create a resonance and a connection to an underlying archetypal constellation operative in the psyches of both client and therapist. All life develops through the creation and development of patterns of resonance. (Dunne and Jahn, 1989) The importance of these patterns is captured in the following:

116

> The concept of resonance as a mechanism for introduc-
> ing order into random physical processes may also be a
> viable model for comprehending various other anomalous
> processes, such as human creativity, whether artistic, intel-
> lectual or biological. The key lies in the mechanics of the
> Indistinguishability principle, where the surrender of the
> distinction between the identities of two interacting sub-
> systems translates into an increment in the structural
> integrity of the bonded system. (79)

Myriad examples of these processes exist. Consider the importance of the parental attitude at the time of a child's conception as
well as the impact of the mother's diet and her physical, emotional,
and spiritual life on the fetus. Ecosystems as well are sensitive systems, affected by their internal morphogenetic dynamics and by the
conditions around them.

The feeling of being either in or out of sync with someone is
common to many of us. Similarly, in looking at how the brain processes new information, we find yet another example of the dynamics of
replication and resonance. Research has taught us that the brain processes and metabolizes a new event through cross-referencing it with
what is already known and has already been experienced. This cross-
referential process produces a resonance between past and current
events. For instance, when we meet someone new at a conference or
at a party, we usually search for some common point of reference.
Possibly we know someone in common or have been interested in
similar things. This cross-referencing makes what was novel familiar
by drawing it into a resonance with past experiences.

These are not humanly contrived, consciously derived operations.
Instead they exist as the psyche or nature's way of making connections
and building relationships. I am suggesting that the same set of dynamics
operative in the biological and social domain also drives processes
occurring within the psyche. While many theorists suggest that the psyche
is modelled after the brain or vice versa, we can eliminate these argu-
ments by collapsing the dualistic separation of mind and body, brain and

psyche. Instead, we may consider that the operations and the information needed for their respective functioning derive from a similar source.

Here we begin moving toward a unitary theory, a consilience, for biological as well as conscious and unconscious functioning. These processes represent a set of natural laws and regularities in the life process operative whenever and wherever evolution occurs. These laws are not confined to one arena. Erich Janstch (1980) makes this same point:

> Science is about to recognize these principles as general laws of the dynamics of nature. Applied to humans and their systems of life, they appear therefore as principles of a profoundly natural way of life. (*The Self Organizing Universe,* 8)

The regularity of pattern repetition speaks to the strength of pre-formed, archetypal constellations that continually manifest and influence individual and collective life. The enduring nature of these patterns and their tendency to introduce the individual to what one could call the destiny factor suggest that archetypal informational fields exist as the central organizing factor in life. It is quite astounding to think of the force of the compulsion to repeat, especially in light of the continued havoc and discomfort such enactment brings. Rather than offer a reductive explanation for this compulsion, we may be better prepared to understand this phenomenon if we look at it as a type of fixed or periodic attractor, drawing the individual into a basin of attraction for an evolutionary, and possibly even a teleological, purpose.

The repetition creates a number of crucial dynamics in the individual's life. The first involves the stabilization of a specific behavioral, archetypal pattern, lived out despite the distress it causes the individual. Second, the repetitive pattern, usually established in early childhood, is lived out in adulthood with a precision that ensures a fidelity and obedience to the original event. Third, because the repetition demands the continual recreation of a specific, relational pattern, it limits the individual's freedom of thought and behavior. Lastly, many new experiences in the individual's life constellate around the nucleus of the replicative-archetypal order, tending to fit the original pattern.

FROM FORM TO CHAOS TO HIGHER FORM

With this notion of order, we move into the confusing realm of deterministic, goal-oriented processes. The crux of Jung's work rests on the premise that the psyche is essentially a self-organizing entity striving to continually unfold according to an innate destiny factor. His notion of directedness is built on an understanding of processes in the natural world where the mature form of a species is often present in its adolescent stage. Here we can speak of a type of archetypal, psychic entelechy.

Drawing from the biological domain, we find Rupert Sheldrake (1981) describing entelechy as: ". . . something which bears its end or goal in itself; it 'contains' the goal towards which a system under its control is directed." (*A New Science of Life,* 46) Citing Hans Driesch's work on entelechy, Sheldrake continues:

> He [Driesch] postulated that entelechy organized and con-
> trolled physicochemical processes during morphogenesis;
> the genes were responsible for providing the material means
> of morphogenesis—the chemical substances to be ordered—
> but the ordering itself was brought about by entelechy. (*A
> New Science of Life,* 45)

From discoveries in systems and evolutionary theories, we find a number of regularities underlying the life process that parallel the human tendency to repeat. On the role of replicative processes, as evidenced in autopoiesis for the development of structure, Erich Janstch writes:

> Autopoiesis refers to the characteristic of living systems to
> continuously renew themselves and to regulate this process
> in such a way that the integrity of their structure is main-
> tained. (*The Self Organizing Universe,* 7).

Life on the cellular level involves autopoietic processes that pro-ceed through a division and replication of the original form. Nature's tendency toward the replication, reproduction, and conservation of patterns serves to inform and ensure the existence of life on all levels.

119

Development involves the organism's "memory of its evolutionary pathways" and a relatively strict replication of these original, informational patterns. Human development obeys a similar set of evolutionary, archetypal laws in that the conception and growth of the fetus closely adhere to a set of morphogenetic regularities. Any alterations in these informationally and morphogenetically coded, developmental stages can be fatal to the life of the organism. Here again we find that near precise replication is not a developmental prerogative so much as nature's imperative. However, for life to proceed from simplicity to complexity, the system must move beyond replication, and with this evolution comes the creation of dissipative structures. Jantsch describes this development:

> A system, which is too small, will always be dominated by the boundary effects. Only beyond certain critical dimensions do the non-linearities find an opportunity to unfold their characteristics and may bring a selection of new structures into play resulting in a certain autonomy of the system with respect to its environment. A dissipative structure comes only into being when a specific size can be realized. (40)

In discussing the role of dissipative structures, we move into thermodynamics and chaos theory. Thermodynamic theory has much to offer our investigation of the repetition. Of interest is the role of entropy, and with the introduction of chaos theory, the creation of negentropic systems. Chaos theory looks at a system's move away from and toward equilibrium and the changes ushered in through these dynamics. From the perspective of thermodynamics, we find a seeming contradiction in that repetition both maintains and disturbs a system's equilibrium. Repetition maintains equilibrium by restricting the degree of freedom and novelty that is allowed to influence growth. On this level we have a movement toward stability. However, on an unconscious level, the continued repetition of a painful pattern causes a considerable amount of anguish and creates a degree of disequilibrium. While the repetition of abuse may be familiar, it is an assault to the soul because meaning, evolution, and novelty are restricted.

In looking at these two aspects of the repetition, it may be help-ful to view the multidimensionality of the human psyche. The conscious and preconscious experience a certain degree of satisfaction in the replicative mode's capacity to bring about familiarity and equi-librium. The unconscious and the individual's relationship to Self and soul, on the other hand, register an assault. Langs (1986) offers an insightful presentation of these dynamics in his discussion of how the mind processes levels of unconscious meaning:

> Those raw images that are deemed by the Message Analyz-ing Center to be anxiety provoking to a point beyond the tolerance of the conscious system are immediately relegated to unconscious processing. ("A New Model of the Mind," 24)

Langs (1986) continues:

> The vast literature on unconscious perception, uncon-scious cognition, and preconscious processing ... amply support the concept of unconscious processing prior to con-scious experience for all incoming information, and the existence of a highly selective filtering and analyzing sys-tem that operates unconsciously prior to conscious experience. ("A New Model of the Mind," 25)

As mentioned earlier, the purpose and evolutionary value embed-ded in repetitive behavior is often lost if the specific behaviors are continually reenacted, rather than understood and converted into mean-ing. There comes a point, however, when the system or individual soul tires of the struggle and moves farther and farther into an entropic (increasing loss of energy) regime—a closed system. The nature of closed systems is that they remain refractory to new information and, in so doing, further subsidize the prior replication. H. Schmeck's work (1974) on the immune system offers an important insight into the effects of unmetabolized repetitive cycles in the body:

> [I]t is almost as though the body finally wearies of the self-nonself argument that [it] has been carrying on with its environment for a lifetime. (*Immunity*, 76)

On an archetypal level, the repetition creates a thermodynamic disequilibrium. At this point in the replicative mode, the human psyche is pushed toward a bifurcation point because of its intrinsic need for growth and meaning making. The individual has the opportunity to use the repetition either as an opportunity for change that will disturb the system and move it towards greater complexity and meaning (negentropy) or to remain in the same replicative cycle.

Describing nonlinear dynamics and the types of processes activated as the system moves from stability to instability, Ervin Laszlo (1987) writes that far-from-equilibrium systems are:

> nonlinear and occasionally indeterminate. They do not tend toward minimum free energy and maximum entropy but may evolve toward a new dynamic regime that is radically different from stationary states at or near equilibrium. (*Evolution,* 21)

As the repetition moves the individual or system into a chaotic phase, the possibility for complexity and greater development is activated. Recall that evolution becomes virtually impossible if the system's parameters remain overly constricted. Behavioral patterns, thoughts, and actions tend to cluster more and more tightly around specific archetypal alignments/themes, thus further diminishing the opportunity for growth. With this clustering around archetypal and informational singularity, we are, developmentally speaking, thrown back to a phylogenetically earlier phase of life. The system simply follows its historical past, rather than developing individual uniqueness. Similar to life at the unicellular level, movement within the replicative mode proceeds through a spinning out of autopoietic, self-similar processes.

Disruption of stability represents a natural phase transition in the life of every system. While we have the continual drive toward self-replication, there is an equally strong movement toward complexity. Continual repetition will eventually result in a deadening of possibilities, thus reinforcing tendencies to remain closed. Janstch provides a concise description of what happens when replicative modelling dominates a system's evolution:

> In contrast to evolutionary feedback, there is no inten-
> sification of the interactions between system and
> environment but their eventual termination instead. (*The
> Self Organizing Universe,* 43)

Freud observed the existence of two seemingly opposing forces within the psyche. The death instinct operates through replication-repetitive cycling, which leaves the system increasingly depleted of energy, while the life instinct moves the system toward higher complexity and the creation of new life. In an extremely interesting observation on the function of the sex drive and its relationship to this forward-moving life instinct, Freud (1915) wrote:

> Let us, however, return to the self-preservative sexual
> instincts. . .. . the coalescence of two individuals which
> separate soon afterwards without any subsequent cell divi-
> sion occurring [which] has a strengthening and rejuvenating
> effect upon both of them. (*Beyond the Pleasure Principle,* 55)

He continued:

> The sphere of embryonic developmental processes is no
> doubt extremely rich in such phenomena of repetition; the
> two germ-cells that are involved in sexual reproduction and
> their life history are themselves only repetitions of the
> beginnings of organic life. But the essence of the processes
> to which sexual life is directed is the coalescence of two
> cell-bodies. That alone is what guarantees the immortality
> of the living substance in the higher organisms. (*Beyond
> the Pleasure Principle,* 56)

Here Freud is describing how self-organizing, replicative processes ensure the development and preservation of the species as well as the creation of diversity within the individual and the collective.

The repetition, if left to endlessly spin within its own cycle and parameters, becomes entropic and eventually dampens the creation of new energy and growth possibilities. Hence the progressive development of chaotic attractors within all systems fueled by archetypal fields. To what end? Perhaps we must shift the paradigm to follow where archetypal field theory leads us.

CHAPTER EIGHT

From Reduction to Induction
Shifting the Paradigm

Repetitive, iterative, and recursive processes occur in almost every area of life. The human fetus develops through the reproduction and duplication of virtually identical cells. It is only in a later phase of human development that cellular diversification and specialization take place. Plants and animals also evolve through iterative processes in which the morphogenetic constants of the species spin out information, dictating specific shadings of form for each organism.

Similarly, in music we often find a repetitive pattern or melody running throughout a piece. In a fascinating project, a researcher at South Florida University translated both the DNA sequence of the AIDS virus and the structure of T-cells into music. The composition that resulted has an unnerving effect on the listener. As we hear the powerful sounds representing the AIDS virus, we are gradually introduced to the musical representation of the T cells a fluttering sound, like a butterfly circling a flower. While hoping for the T-cells' victory over the destructive AIDS virus, unfortunately we hear their painful death cries instead. Their initially clear, fluttering sounds slow down and in the end stop, with only the seemingly unending melody of the AIDS virus remaining. The strength of the virulent cells is too painfully apparent.

One of the difficulties in combating AIDs is the fact that there is little repetition in its genetic coding. In this experiment, it took almost five pages of sheet music before a repetitive pattern emerged in the DNA sequencing of the AIDS virus. We see how in the absence of repetition, the body becomes unable to counteract disease. A more familiar replicative code, like one of a common virus, allows the body to recognize the specifics of the disorder and create an antibody to counteract the viral infection. In large measure, the repetition serves as a memory coding and informational retrieval system for the body, allowing for the recognition and activation of appropriate healing agents. Thus repetition proves its value even on a cellular level.

The important point is that for life to evolve and develop, a series of fundamental habits of nature—archetypal and morphogenetic—must unfold in a recursive manner to ensure the growth of a system. Consciousness and self-reflection, which are non-repetitive and non-instinctive, are latecomers to human experience and are predated by these autonomous laws.

While variation and diversity are equally important players in the evolution of life, nevertheless they emerge almost always after an iterative, replicative process has been established. Recursive processes occur first to insure the stability of form, and to accomplish this goal, the system must remain refractory to the emergence of new information that could disrupt its autopoietic, self-replicating regime. Nonetheless, a certain degree of openness is always present in the system as evidenced by its relationship to environmental stimuli.

For instance, I have a ten-year-old cactus plant on my office desk. One of its arms is supported by a horizontal desk shelf, and this arm grows parallel to the shelf. Another arm has climbed over the shelf and grows toward the window. The arm supported by the shelf grows in somewhat regular, incremental stages, each new section closely matching the previous one in size and spacing. In contrast, the unsupported arm shows a much more irregular growth pattern. Its sections vary more in size and, to some extent, even in shape. And, because it is not supported by the desk shelf, it is more strongly influenced by the gravitational pull of the earth as it grows down toward the ground.

While sections of the cactus plant are quite different from one another, the overall design of the plant is obvious and recognizable to anyone. Undeniably though, while the morphogenetic information and field influencing its growth remain relatively consistent, a degree of variation continues to exist in its growth pattern. This variation suggests that while the morphogenetic constraints of a system pull it toward a functionally closed regime, it still retains a degree of openness to environmental influences, such as the sun, water, gravity, and perhaps the emotional ambiance of the room itself, etc. Within constancy of form, we find a degree of openness to the larger surrounding fields present in the environment, confirming that world and psyche are open, creative systems.

Evolution requires that a relationship between an organism and its environment be established if life is to be sustained. Every species, every culture, every tribe becomes intimately related to its environment. The Inuits, for instance, whose survival depends on the ability to read patterns in the snow and ice, have developed an extensive vocabulary to describe the many different states of snow, while most languages offer but one or two words for it. Desert people learn innovative and often astonishing ways of finding water in a seemingly parched land. Without exception, every animal's physiology reflects its adaptation to environmental challenges common to its species. And, in virtually every case, we find the establishment of a resonance between the environment and the individual organism, the container and the contained, that is pivotal to the growth process. Perhaps Mae-Wan Ho's belief that health is only found in coherent systems is fundamental and reflects what is needed for the development and continuance of generativity and life.

Every organism and environment will naturally resonate with that which is habitual and familiar. The habitual is most often identical to repetitive behavior. Yet, at a certain point, the failure to move beyond familiarity halts evolution. Evolution and life, like the T-cells struggling for survival and victory, will not be denied without a struggle. In some way, and for some overarching purpose, the archetypal fields at play in any given relationship will cause movement toward the establishment of a new pattern. Such a pivotal transition within a system is termed by Rene Thom "an information catastrophe," which is described as:

127

> the results of the actions of active information carriers
> which interfere with the replicative cycles of the social
> system, upsetting its organization ... catastrophes lead to
> functional changes which interrupt or destroy parts of the
> organization. (*Structural Stability and Morphogenesis,* 3)

As the system encounters a catastrophe, it enters a third state, far-from-equilibrium field. When the habitual is suddenly punctuated by what is novel (Stephen J. Gould's notion of punctuated equilibria), it is thrown into chaos by the introduction of the information catastrophe. As we now understand from chaos theory, nonlinear dynamics, and from Ervin Laszlo's work in "General and Dynamical Systems Theory," complexity arises in response to a system's move from either equilibrium or non-equilibrium to a far-from-equilibrium position. Laszlo (1987) describes the far-from-equilibrium state as follows:

> The third possible state of systems is the state far from ther-
> mal and chemical equilibrium. Systems in this state are
> nonlinear and occasionally indeterminate. They do not tend
> toward minimum free energy and maximum entropy but
> may amplify certain fluctuations and evolve toward a new
> dynamic regime that is radically different from stationary
> states at or near equilibrium. (*Evolution,* 21)

Just as the phoenix bursts into flames so that it may rise anew and immortal from its ashes—winged, soaring creature that it is—it appears that all life endures the encoded partial destruction of key elements at special moments to insure evolution.

In discussing the existence of patterns and their archetypal roots, it becomes obvious that a strong parallel exists between Jung's work and that of modern physics and field theory. Jung's description of the complex serves us well in the investigation of archetypal pattern recognition. The complex, according to Jung, exists as highly charged quanta of energy organized around an archetypal core. He speaks of the existence of a certain magnetic pull operative within the complex's field, working to create resonances between its archetypal core and like experiences in the outer world. Synchronicities and similar phe-

128

nomena are experiences of the relationship between the internal archetypal constellation, or complex, and its manifestation in the outer world. F. David Peat (1987) makes this point:

> It is as if the formation of patterns within the uncon-
> scious mind is accompanied by physical patterns in the outer
> world ... certain events in the universe cluster together into
> meaningful patterns without recourse to the normal pushes
> and pulls of causality. (*Synchronicity*, 27, 35)

As the above quotation suggests, the psyche tunes into and possibly even creates informational, archetypal fields that serve as the orientational backdrop out of which individual experience evolves. These fields and their respective representations in form are manifested through the clustering of events, effects, and synchronicities in personal and collective experience. Seeking to identify the matrix out of which these changes evolve, F. David Peat (1987) draws on the Hamilton-Jacobi Theory as a possible explanation:

> [T]his new form of dynamics shows that all motion and
> change emerge out of a "law of the whole" and that the
> patterns and events of nature are the expression of an
> underlying unity of form. (*Synchronicity*, 55)

This "underlying unity of form" may be equated with the archetypal field, which matches David Bohm's idea of the explicate world of matter being created out of the implicate order.

As we gain a deeper appreciation and ability to recognize these patterns, our next task is to create a classification of archetypal fields and develop the capacity to recognize the clustering of events, configurations, and phenomena unique to each archetype. Alex Andrews (1989) makes a similar point in suggesting that

> ... pattern classification is a better term [than pattern rec-
> ognition], so that the word pattern can refer to a
> configuration of input data, to be "recognized" or classi-
> fied. (*Self Organizing Systems*, 50)

129

Pattern recognition and pattern classification have already played a crucial role in the development of artificial intelligence. A number of computers are programmed to play games like chess and checkers. From the individual moves in the game, these programs identify the larger patterns out of which the moves arise and then calculate the most probable and best possible response.

Since 9/11, the news has been filled with stories about the importance of reading patterns. For instance, we have learned that the pilots who crashed into The Trade Center paid for their flight lessons with cash. Additionally, and perhaps even more striking, was the finding that one of the suspected terrorists told his flight instructor that he only needed to learn to take off, but not to land. Apparently, the CIA and FBI were informed about these events but felt that that they were not a sufficient cause for alarm.

When we realize that life is dependent on our capacity to read patterns—and now we can especially understand the consequences of not being able to do so accurately—the time is ripe in our personal and collective experience to take heed of the patterns existing around us. As stated above, each detail, like each symptom, is part of a larger whole. So again we see how the whole can be inferred from the parts.

Biological systems are also governed to a large extent by the same principles of pattern recognition and classification. Andrews describes various operations—from the retinal activity in the frog to the body's ability to maintain health—as stemming from the capacity to recognize patterns and to respond accordingly. For instance, the frog's retinal processing system is maximally excited when the pattern presented has a light-dark edge. Andrews goes on to say that in order for the frog to catch bugs:

> an appropriate response . . . must depend on post-retinal integration of the outputs from the sustained contrast detectors and moving edge detectors. (*Self-Organizing Systems,* 74)

We thus see how even the frog's survival is dependent on its ability to recognize patterns.

FROM REDUCTION TO INDUCTION

I am only beginning to learn about a number of other interesting discoveries and advances in the field of pattern classification. The concept and creation of the "perceptron," for example, holds great promise in furthering our understanding of fields and patterns. As described by Andrews:

> The term perceptron was coined by Rosenblatt (1959, 1961) to refer to a class of devices capable of learning to classify patterns . . . . The device is usually described as a scheme or visual pattern classification, but it can also be used for other modalities ... it can be used for word recognition, for example. (*Self Organizing Systems,* 134)

Clearly, the need to recognize, classify, and respond to the existence of patterns is important for survival on all levels. It is increasingly clear that the human psyche also works through the creation, recognition, and identification of archetypal patterns in nature and human psyche. To comprehend these fields and their physical representations more fully, we benefit greatly by developing an appreciation for interdisciplinary studies, including biology, systems theory, chaos theory, nonlinear dynamics, Jungian analysis, organizational theory, and theology. All address basic patterns found in the world that are responsible for the generation of matter and form. Interestingly enough, chaos theory and nonlinear dynamics describe the transition from a highly patterned behavior to the emergence of new order and complexity.

If we seriously consider the implications of an archetypal, informational field theory, we are led to view life as evolving through the creation of recursive processes and then moving forward into new domains. Through maintaining constancy with the conservative laws of nature and the original archetypal and morphogenetic principles responsible for the generation of life, diversity and complexity eventually evolve into the myriad cultural, physical, and botanical forms that exist in the world.

Jung's work on the nature of the psyche, most particularly his theory of the archetypes, was ahead of its time. Late in life he began a collaborative relationship with Wolfgang Pauli, the internationally recognized physicist, that extended even further his investigations into the nature of the psyche. Jung realized that if we were to deepen our comprehension of the psyche and the working of archetypal phenomena, we must inaugurate a series of interdisciplinary studies. Marie-Louise von Franz (1992) also makes this point:

> To clarify these creative possibilities [of better understanding the psyche], we would like to have a group of physicists who are willing to take on a deep Jungian analysis—not because we want to rule them or influence them—we desire simply that they learn. And then we would have to have a few Jungian analysts who would take the trouble to study physics. I think that's what first would have to be done, so that both knew really deeply the other's subject. (*Psyche and Matter*, 162)

In investigating the underlying ways and habits of matter in the outer world, we gain access to the archetypes from which they emerge. If our quest for understanding is not fueled by a sense of awe and respect for these processes, the work itself will eventually grow arid. Investigations about the world and the realization that the world we see reflects the workings of the psyche, or of some previously unknown self-organizing potential, are the most exciting undertakings imaginable. I hope that in some synchronistic, synergistic way this book helps us to make further headway in understanding how psyche works. Finally, we may all have to admit that while studying and thinking about these ideas are essential, we are ultimately touching phenomena infinitely greater than personal consciousness. Perhaps in our continuing quest to understand the deeper dimensions of psyche, we can find meaning in Teilhard de Chardin's musing that "matter is spirit moving slowly enough to be seen." (qtd in Fagg, 95)

CHAPTER NINE

Further Dimensions of Confluence

A rchetypal fields organize behavior by creating complementary relationships within their area of influence.
The constellation of an archetype functions as a stable or
periodic attractor, ushering in material from these *a priori* fields. This
orients the individual to a set of experiences and influences that are
synonymous with the nature of the activated archetype. Here we have
an important coupling between Jung and the new sciences. Jung looks
at archetypes as products of nature that whether consciously apprehended or not, still affect human consciousness. Marie-Louise von
Franz similarly sees archetypes as "nature's constants." The new sciences extend investigations into subtle influences in the natural world
by looking at the nature of fields. Fields, like electromagnetic and
gravitational ones, also affect human consciousness. Robert Becker
has conducted numerous studies on the physiological effects of electromagnetic frequencies. And, Lawrence Fagg, in *Electromagnetism
and the Sacred,* describes how light is a product of electromagnetism.
He posits a direct correlation between light and spiritual insight, noting that spiritual experiences historically are accompanied by the
presence of a striking luminescence.

Having a singular alignment to an archetype is analogous to having access to just one room in a multi-leveled house. Then, as
complexity develops, the individual realizes the existence of other
previously undiscovered rooms. The movement from realization to
discovery to assimilation often necessitates the building of a relationship, an introjective experience, with someone who has access to these

other rooms. This new person serves as a representative and ambassador of a wider and greater field of influence by carrying information and features from these other rooms into consciousness. This creates the necessary conditions for change, where with increased understanding and guidance, movement can occur that allows one to have a broader experience of an archetypal field. The singular alignment to just one aspect of an archetype and its potential teleology may then be understood and its possessive hold on the personality broken as increased knowledge, experience, and information become available.

The implications of archetypal field theory for individual experience and our global society are profound. Fields influence human experiences, societies, and even entire countries, which may unknowingly respond to their mandates. Consider the situation in Germany under Hitler's regime as an illustration of the tremendous influence fields can have on a nation. Through the embodiment of Hitler as leader, an entire country was moved to actions it would have never committed if it had not been possessed by powerful archetypal and unconscious content.

In 1918, even before the outbreak of war in Europe, Jung observed

> an astonishing development in the German edition of the collective unconscious. I had caught hold of certain collective dreams of Germans which convinced me that they portrayed the beginning of a national regression ... I saw Nietzsche's "blond beast" looming up with all that it implies. I felt sure that Christianity would be challenged and that the Jews would be taken to account. (*CW 18*, § 1322)

Based on his understanding of the power of archetypal constellations in the unconscious and their progression from potential to actual experience, Jung suggested that efforts might be made to "start the discussions (with German leaders) in order to forestall the inevitable violence of the unconscious outburst . . ." (*CW 18*, § 1322)

Nations and groups alike organize in response to transpersonal influences. The fate of a nation under the sway of a field is potentially devastating due to the masses directly affected by its dynamics. Jung, in 1936, commented that:

> Nations being the largest organized groups are from a psychological point of view clumsy, stupid, and amoral monsters .... The psychology of masses is always inferior .... The whole of a nation never reacts like a normal individual, but always like a primitive group being .... They are inaccessible to reasonable arguments, they are suggestible like hysterical patients, they are childish and moody, helpless victims of their emotions. (*CW 18*, § 1315)

The events in Nazi Germany are part of our painful collective history, and we are once again facing dangerous collective and national identifications with archetypal fields, as evidenced by the recent wars in Bosnia, the continuing slaughter in various parts of Africa, and the ongoing atrocities in the Middle East. It is hard to believe that today, when we already have been so affected by the ravages of violence, humanity continues to engage in warfare where the most brutal acts of indignity are committed. Each day we hear about babies in Africa hacked to pieces with machetes. Bosnian people are forced to endure tortures similar to those inflicted in Nazi concentration camps, and enemy troops are incinerated. The perseverance of violence throughout history begs the question: "What do we really know about human behavior and morality?"

Perhaps we can begin by admitting that war is a universal, archetypal phenomenon that has occurred in virtually every culture since the beginning of time. If this is in fact the case, we have to look beyond its temporal manifestations to determine the goal and meaning embedded in this ferocious and seemingly insatiable archetype. In most instances, war occurs in response to growing tensions between opposing forces, each despising what the other stands for. Each side projects its own inferiorities and shadows onto the other.

Political and global conflicts also may be better understood by viewing them as the workings of archetypal fields. A number of years ago, while visiting Canada, I saw the influence of archetypal fields in Quebec's efforts toward independence. In a television interview, Jean Charest, the Leader of the Liberal Party of Quebec, explained that the central issue was not for Quebec simply to externalize its fight for succession. Instead, its people should bring to consciousness how they are in fact different and unique from the rest of Canada and be proud of their distinct identity. His comments were brilliant because he asked the people to acknowledge and metabolize the archetypal aspects of their situation rather than engage in a mass political movement. He wanted the people to appreciate their own unique identity, tradition, language, and culture.

Clearly, there are times when outer world changes are needed. However, we all too frequently treat the outer manifestation of a problem and ignore its underlying archetypal significance. In our example from Canada, we can infer that the archetypal constellation involved issues of independence and separation. In articulating the nature of the constellated archetype that compelled Quebecois into action, Charest worked in much the same manner as Jung would work with an individual possessed by an archetype—he encouraged the people to metabolize the issue that was at the core of the archetypal possession, which concerned the meaning of separation and independence. In the absence of a personal response to an archetype, possession is a likely outcome. In creating a differentiated and conscious response, however, a meaningful alliance is established between ego and archetype or, in this case, between culture and archetype.

This point is further illustrated by recent events in the Middle East. Fatalities among border guards are well known in some areas. To counteract this bloodshed, it was recommended that border guards wear nametags listing pertinent personal information—age, number of children, etc. After the introduction of these personalized nametags, border patrol fatalities dropped to virtually zero. This suggests that the atrocities of war can only occur when individuals and nations are possessed by an archetypal and collective fervor. The archetypal absorbs the personal and entrains the individual or nation to the constellated archetype. In a paper written with a colleague Judith Rossi (1998), we addressed the issue of collective possession:

> It is well recognized that virtually every culture, from ancient to modern, has an established set of rituals and ritualistic behaviors to insure the transition from personal to collective functioning. For instance, a primitive tribe may use repetitive drumming to induce a trance-like state in warriors preparing for battle. From ancient armies to modern forces, the phenomena of entire groups of infantry marching in perfect formation serves the same purpose. The goal is to entrain the individual perspective with the collective, so that the group may perform assignments untenable or even repugnant to the individual. ("Archetypal Dimensions of Territoriality," 3)

In our earlier example, archetypal possession was broken by the ingenious introduction of nametags. Suddenly, anonymous soldiers, whose identities and tasks were archetypal (to overcome an equally impersonal archetypal enemy), became individuals with homes, families, and children. No longer were they merely a faceless enemy to be eliminated. What had been purely archetypal—the enemy, the projection of evil onto others—had now achieved individual distinction.

This projection-making process is also a common occurrence in the therapeutic domain. Clinicians have developed a number of useful ways to help clients understand these dynamics. The most important is modelling for the client how to better recognize and accept responsibility for the contents of projected, evacuated, and discarded emotions. Then, through reflection and assimilation, the individual hopefully becomes able to withdraw his or her projections and see them as reflecting contents from his or her own psyche. Perhaps we can begin our renewed efforts at peace negotiations by applying a similar approach at the national and global levels.

Individuals react with hatred and violence in response to something greater than individual consciousness—they have become possessed by an archetype. Even in those instances when violence is invoked in the name of God and goodness, it reflects the embodiment of evil. History reminds us that the religious Crusades resulted in the deaths of hundreds of thousands of people. In the recent Scorcese film *Gangs of New York*, the son of a slain Christ-like figure seeks to avenge his father's death against Bill the Butcher, who represents the Antichrist. As the two prepare for hand-to-hand battle, knowing that probably only one of them will come out alive, each prays to his God for help in slaying the other, the enemy. To have a notorious butcher of men praying to "his God" for strength in battle is an act of madness. So too, however, is it madness to prepare to kill your nemesis.

The genre of war movies takes up a similar theme, as evidenced in films like *Apocalypse Now, Platoon,* and *The Killing Fields.* The images are otherworldly, and the soldiers' experiences are beyond anything we could ever imagine enduring. So, while some of the archetypal objectives and goals behind war, like the need to liberate the oppressed, may be necessary for a country's advancement and survival, the national, collective response and possession by these forces is virtually psychotic in that individual egos are lost to the collective movement. More importantly, we know only too well of the human casualties resulting from these identifications. As war fuels the escalation of primitive emotions, the teleological hope for understanding that lies behind such enactments is lost.

I believe that an appreciation of field phenomena may help us translate and convert these unconscious behaviors into opportunities for greater understanding. An awareness of an "archetypal morphology" and the capacity to see the formation of transpersonal patterns may help us recognize movements that all too often lead to national and global catastrophes. Perhaps with this knowledge we may develop useful intervention strategies to stave off future eruptions of violence. Our newly formed Assisi Foundation is planning a conference about the archetypal dimensions of war and peace and will draw an internationally recognized faculty from the fields of theology, Jungian psychology, international diplomacy, and the new sciences for its inaugural program. However, with such a wretched history of failed peace attempts, we may have to maintain the image of peace as an internal reality.

The continuing study of the effects and workings of archetypal fields brings yet another potential benefit to humanity. By acknowledging that fields are transpersonally, and not personally, generated, we can begin to reestablish a relationship between ego consciousness and the transpersonal. In this regard, we may need to more carefully define consciousness. Traditionally, consciousness has been viewed as a function and product of our perceptions. We are conscious—that is, aware that something has entered our perceptual field. However, recent findings in the area of consciousness research confirm Jung's original view of the psyche and extend the definition of consciousness beyond the realm of perceptual influences. For instance, in the world of computers, it has been said that at any given moment there are one hundred bits of information available to be apprehended and processed. Yet the human mind, while capable of processing and storing huge quantities of information, generally processes only 7.4% of incoming material, leaving the remaining 92.6% still in the shadows of the unconscious where it will continue exerting its influence.

Perhaps we also can extend the definition of consciousness to encompass the magnitude of those experiences where personal consciousness extends into the transpersonal dimension. Clearly, phenomena such as synchronicities, the human capacity to heal at a distance, and the telepathic transfer of information involve more than cognitive and perceptual abilities. Here we have an immersion into a deeper, more open, and knowledgeable dimension of the psyche that may even transcend mind/brain functioning. I stress the need to expand our notions of consciousness because as we continue to learn about the powers of the mind and brain, we may create an unnecessary schism between mind, or consciousness, and the unconscious.

Laszlo (1996) makes a similar point regarding the potentially damaging effects of such dualities when discussing his views on current world problems. He suggests that we have gone too far in our valuation of individualism and human difference and that our desperate attempt to affirm individual and national identities has jeopardized our capacity to recognize personal and global interconnectivity. He discusses the tremendous degree of interpenetrability existing in the world, where many of the barriers and boundaries we create are, in a fundamental sense, false divisions within a unified world. To acknowledge the presence and power of archetypal fields brings the message of a unified world back into human consciousness. Individuals and nations have unique and separate identities that should be respected. However, to linger in the affirmation of difference speaks to our fear of connection and denies our embeddedness in something more profound and powerful.

Neumann (1954) also realized the limitations of our egocentric, personal, and collective development:

> The collective unconscious of mankind must be experienced and apprehended by the consciousness of mankind as the ground common to all men. Not until the differentiation into races, nations, tribes, and groups has, by a process of integration, been resolved in a new synthesis, will the danger of recurrent invasions from the unconscious be averted. (*Origins and History of Consciousness,* 418)

He calls for a profound paradigmatic shift that could usher in the realization of the unified background described by Bohm, Jung, Laszlo, and others:

> A future humanity will then realize the center, which the individual personality today experiences as his own self-center, to be one with humanity's very self . . . (*Origins and History of Consciousness* 418)

Native American culture has a better understanding and respect for the interconnected universe. Linguistic scholars have found that many Native American languages and dialects rarely have a word for "mine;" instead the collective "ours" is more commonly used. In fact, the first time I treated a Native American in analysis, I found this "mine/ours" distinction confusing. Whenever my client discussed events and situations about colleagues and family, I was often left wondering "who said what to whom" because the words, phrasing, and descriptions lacked the differentiation found in European culture. Fortunately, in time I understood his communicative style as expressive of his Native American background and psyche. Many of his cultural and religious practices also echoed this sense of commonality and shared experience. His culture's relationship with the earth was one of respect, and the belief that people and the earth are part of the same fabric of life was a central doctrine.

Many of my findings from analyzing the therapeutic situation reveal a similar underlying connectedness. Therapist and client tend to function as a single entity at significant moments in treatment. Here the boundaries between the therapist's private thoughts and dreams and those of the client become entwined and entrained, functioning as a synchronized dyad, each responding to a shared archetypal field. Robert Langs' works (1976, 1982, 1986) on the interactional field in psychotherapy represent pivotal breakthroughs in our understanding of these shared fields. However innovative his work is, it has not addressed the underlying goal and meaning of this synchronization. This is where my own research has picked up the thread. I have found that the resonance patterns, coherence, and synchronization created in the interactional field function as primary vehicles for healing and for the creation of greater complexity.

The idea of a transpersonal dimension has been with us since the beginning of civilization. Every nation and culture has recognized the presence of non-personally acquired influences as evidenced through the universality of the god concept. As cultures have revered the relationship between the individual and the transpersonal, we too need to find some way for including it again in our notions of consciousness. In this way, we create the opportunity to reconnect to the generative matrix of human and global experience.

As stated throughout this book, the capacity to recognize and understand the meaning of archetypal fields offers important opportunities for resolving conflicts on the personal and collective, or global, levels. The significance of this approach is recognized in diverse fields, including psychology, the natural sciences, the arts, organizational development, and international politics. As an example, I have recently been approached by a group of highly regarded organizational consultants to discuss the workings of archetypal fields and archetypal pattern recognition. Similarly, I have been contacted by a foreign diplomat to assist in his country's lingering problems with boundary disputes. He explained that, after hearing my lecture on field phenomena and the workings of archetypal fields, he immediately realized their applicability to his country's conflicts. I have learned that Andrew Samuels and other Jungian analysts have been working to help resolve the political struggles between Great Britain and Ireland. Clearly, the time is ripe to apply our understanding of archetypal dynamics to global concerns.

However, the first step in facilitating change may not involve active interventions. Interventions emerge from a matrix of internal dynamics, and not vice versa. This point is well made in the following story. It was during the Nazi uprisings that Jung held a seminar for a group of his most promising students. In it, Jung was chided for not taking an active role in preventing the war. The students felt that since they had learned so much about the human psyche, its tendencies, habits, and potential for health, they should apply their skills to help the peace efforts. Jung was asked, "What should we do to help?" No response came. Asked again the question, he again seemed to ignore it. Then, during the third try, he interrupted them saying that he had to get a pebble out of his shoe. They continued questioning him and finally asked why he would not answer. "I just did," Jung said, explaining that the pebble in his shoe was symbolic of our need to deal with personal evil and destruction and not to simply see them as separate, isolated events in the outer world. In attending to our personal psychological health, we potentially could help a greater

142

number of people than if we were to go off in a missionary zeal to save and redeem the world, while our internal home was in shambles.

There is a limit to Jung's thinking here, but he was correct to work toward the creation and strengthening of a collective resonance around personal psychic integration. As individuals develop their ability to create internal change and order, we may in turn see an exponential increase in our collective ability to change.

Jung's advice for preparing the internal state has a rich, spiritual tradition. Here he follows the sage advice found in the Chinese tale of the rainmaker, who despite the taunts and disappointment of the rain-starved villagers, remained in his hut for four days before emerging to the sudden downpour of rain. He too understood the necessity of internal readiness as a prerequisite for political, social, and climatic change in the world.

Afterthoughts

There is beauty in the world. There are the smells and rhythms of the seasons, the richness of cultural and geographic diversity, and the interesting lives of those around us, which we can see if we only take the time to look and listen to their stories. Sometimes, when I see the juxtaposition of beauty and violence in the world, I wish I could be idealistic and ask why is there such hatred, or freely sing the popular 60s refrain, "Why can't there be peace"? Growing up the way I did on the streets of Brooklyn I learned to be a survivor and, hopefully, to prosper. Neither is accomplished by cockeyed optimism. As children of Italian immigrant families from Sicily and Salerno, my parents understood firsthand the fury of poverty and oppression, the brutishness of cultural bigotry, and a worldview framed by scarcity. The Great Depression had a way of bringing everyone, especially immigrant families, to their knees. My father had to share a bed with four brothers, while the evening's dinner of *anguila* (eel) waited in the family's one bathtub to be served as the sacrificial meal. Most times, my grandfather Eugenio, caught this *capitano* on the shores off

Bay Ridge. He preferred fishing the "old way," which meant that he dropped a line with a hook in the water and held it in his hands—no rod and reel. They knew tough times, and as their children and grand-children, we too learned the art of survival.

Now as an aging baby boomer and a registered member of AARP, I look at the world from a very different vantage point from when I was younger and even from when I wrote the earlier edition of this book three years ago. Now that I am fifty years old, more than half my life is behind me, and I hope to God I can live the remaining years in concert with what is my destiny. I recall one very special moment in our Assisi, Italy Conference a few years back when I asked Mario Jacoby, one of the most senior and respected Jungian analysts in the world, "what have you learned from all your years of studying and living a life influenced by Jung's view of the Self?" He replied with grace and simplicity that he had learned to trust the wisdom of the greater Self and not to let the ego get in its way. Mario is a beautiful man whose friendship I value deeply.

After 9/11, a colleague Jane Carr, who has run a daycare center in New Jersey for more than twenty-five years, said that she felt that perhaps the greatest loss from this tragedy was our children's sense of innocence. America now has caught up with the rest of the world in having to live with terrorism and violence as daily fare. She is right in her reading of its impact on our children. When I have to board a plane for a trip, my son Christopher is always a bit worried and too happy for words when he sees me return home. Planes are not so safe either. He knows this, as so many of today's youth have known losses no children should ever experience. We both acknowledge this reality on a daily basis and incorporate it into our lives.

Collectively, our response to terror and threats is similar to how bacteria becomes increasingly more immune to antibiotics. Our collective psyche creates greater and greater defenses—psychological antigens aimed at staving off vital truths that beckon us daily. When considering our national reaction to 9/11 and the myopic vision we showed in failing to understand the deeper meaning and implications of it, I was moved to write a brief piece stating, " If there is a hell, the price of admission is a life lived as a lie." We seem to have to conceal the truth in order to survive. For years, I have been speaking about the omnipresence of denial and its ravages on the personal and collective psyche. So too, Robert Langs (2000) speaks of our inability to fully face our own death anxiety, and in order to subsidize the cauterizing of our wounds, we live half-lives—lives characterized by the unconscious need to smell the stench of our wounds and in fear of touching what could be beautiful. Marie-Louise von Franz teaches that in order to fully know life, one must fully know death. There is no room for half-truths if we want to live a conscious life. Conscious of what? Of the power of the deep unconscious to move and shape personal lives and nations.

After a bitterly cold winter here in Vermont, where morning temperatures hovered at fifteen below zero, we are ready for spring. We have seen snow for seven months, and many of us are thinking of heading south for warmer waters. Nature must have known that we couldn't tolerate any more cold, snow, and ice and finally brought us the gift of spring. I am finishing the new version of this book two days after Easter. Our family celebrated this glorious, sun-filled, seventy-degree day with friends and family. As is the tradition in Italian families, we opened the barrel of this year's new homemade wine and toasted the old for what we had and for new beginnings. After storing the wine in aged oak barrels for seven months, it is time to let it out and for us to see how our hands, time, and Bacchus have shaped this year's flavors.

I can honestly say that there is now love and a bit more gentleness in my life. With my family, we move forward into the world grateful for what we have found together and very aware of the tenuousness of life. A colleague Enzo Schiano from Naples described a new Italian movie entitled *Casomai*—Italian for "just in case," referring to our tendency to always be on the look out for a way out of a situation. However, Sartre has taught us that there is "No Exit;" we have to live in a world filled with many different emotions and dynamics, all demanding attention from which there is no escape.

So, I have to ask where am I now, after more than twenty-five years of studying this material? More in awe than ever of the dynamism of the psyche. The world of subjectivity is interesting, but pales in comparison to the innate wisdom of the psyche and the wonders of the natural world. We can spend days, months, and eons working to create ourselves, only to find in the end that we are not really the architects of what James Hollis terms "This Journey We Call Life." Subjectivity tells us something valuable about our personal dynamics, but really nothing about the innate dynamics that shape life. I can tell you my feelings about the coming of spring, and these are surely important. However, there is something equally, if not more, compelling about nature's understanding of the cyclical nature of life. We react to these natural rhythms in significant, and perhaps even poetic, ways. Our reactions are our brushstrokes, painted against the backdrop of a frame provided by nature. The world is peopled with individuals, but we did not make the world. We interact with the world every day and bring our own ideas, perceptions, and visions to the table, yet need to realize that the table, in some fundamental sense, may have been waiting for us to decorate it and fill it with the tastes and textures from our own cultures and imaginations. Just think of the spring and summer herbs and vegetables found in beautiful gardens and fruit markets. I wait all winter for the tastes and aromas of fresh basil, parsley, garlic, and tomatoes. Add a bit of fresh mozzarella, and we have a captivating meal of *capresse*. However, while we can choose our own favorite way of working with these ingredients, their innate, natural, and unique flavors nevertheless remain constant. Whether we undercook or overcook the garlic, the nature of garlic remains the same. I think the mystics, and now the homeopaths and naturopaths, know these same truths.

I am guardedly hopeful. Not for the belief in world peace but in the hope that incrementally, small bands of pioneers will gain a foothold, maybe inch by inch in the world. Not much progress when we realize the immensity of the world, but the march forward continues.

FURTHER DIMENSIONS OF CONFLUENCE

I have recently discovered the meaning of the name of the famous Eranos Conferences, where Jung and many of the world's greatest scholars gathered on the shores of *Lago Maggiore* on the border of Northern Italy and Switzerland to discuss the emergent properties of psyche. The word *eranos* refers to a meal where everyone brings something of value to the table. My table has been well fed with the work of colleagues and friends. Some of the most creative personalities of our time have dined at this table, sharing ever so graciously their gifts. To my son, who continually amazes us with his insatiable need to create art, and to all the loved ones in my life, I thank you from the bottom of my heart. What a trip this has been—what a feast. I only hope that in some small way the ideas in this book contribute something to your meal.

Glossary

COMPILED
BY
Anna E. O'Brien (AO), Jyoti Jayaraman (JJ), and Marianne Stigum (MS)

Archetype: (Greek, *archetypon*, model or pattern) (Latin, *archetyp (um)*, an original). An ancient term rescued and preserved from a nearly forgotten antiquity by Carl Jung, who defined it as a universal, transpersonal, and pre-existent pattern guiding form and development. According to Jung, an archetype cannot be examined directly, but evidence of its existence can be found in its effects. He envisioned archetypes as rooted in our instinctual ancestral past and harbored in the collective unconscious. (AO)

Archetypal Field: An energetic component of an archetype, which exerts its influence over space and time. In contrast to fields in the outer world which are space-time dependent, such as gravitational and electromagnetic fields, archetypal fields are non-local and evident in such curious occurrences as telepathy, synchronicity, and other non-local transmissions of information. An understanding of the patterning process of archetypal fields is most valuable in the practice of psychotherapy and all manner of human relationship. (AO)

Autopoesis: (Greek: *auto,* meaning self or same, and *poesis,* meaning production). A property of living organisms to self-complete as evidenced by such processes as regeneration, reproduction, and healing. Autopoesis shows the consistent stabilization of form by way of replicative structures. Both autopoesis and morphogenesis can be seen as processes insuring stabilization of form. These stabilizing factors are intrinsic to a system and will emerge in spite of the ego's efforts to the contrary. (AO)

Chreode: The British biologist C. H. Waddington suggested an extension of the idea of the morphogenetic field to take into account the temporal aspect of development. He called this new concept the *chreode* (from the Greek *chre,* it is necessary, and *hodos,* route or path. (Sheldrake, 50). In simple terms, we can call it a biological pathway or a habit. Brian Goodwin, another British biologist and Assisi conference presenter in 1993 (Assisi, Italy), sees the morphogenetic fields and chreodes as eternally given archetypes (Sheldrake, 236). (MS) Sheldrake, Rupert: *A New Science of Life* (1995). Park Street Press.

Complex: Jung derived his idea of the existence of the complex through the word association test. In giving a list of words to individuals, he found that certain words in the list evoked delayed responses which appeared to be loaded with feeling tone and were indicative of significant conflict in the patients' lives. He called these complexes and found that they could be either positive or negative and reflected important aspects of intrapsychic life. They also appear to be independent of any conscious awareness on the part of the individual carrying them. The critical features of a complex are that they appear to be associated with an archetype, influence behavior, and remain outside a person's conscious awareness. Jung gave the following explanation:

> It is the image of a certain psychic situation which is strongly accentuated emotionally and is, moreover, incompatible with the habitual attitude of consciousness. This image has a powerful inner coherence, it has its own wholeness and, in addition, a relatively high degree of autonomy. . . and therefore behaves like an animated foreign body in the sphere of consciousness. (*CW* 8 § 201) (JJ).

Derivatives: A term coined by Freud. . . It was delineated by Robert Langs who developed the Comunicative Approach in psychotherapy. This term refers to the content in the material communicated between patient and therapist. It is relevant to all communication between people in that there is a recognition that communication can have both latent and manifest content. Manifest verbal and non-verbal communication carries a hidden meaning. It remains the task of the listener to ascertain the nature of this hidden communication. This is done by attending to the patient's stories which carry embedded perceptions and beliefs which are made manifest through metaphors. In his work on the listening process, Langs further subdivides these into Type I and II derivatives and Type A, B, C communication. It is noted that derivatives are deeply held perceptions and beliefs activated by the language of the primary process. They are more readily detectable in stories when they are less defended against. In such instances, they are referred to as "close derivatives." When derivative communication is defended more unconsciously the derivatives are difficult to understand and are referred to as "distant derivatives." (JJ) Berns, U. (2000) *Glossary of Communicative terms*. Langs, R. *This Listening Process*.

Entrainment: A physics phenomenon of resonance, first observed in the 17th century. The history of entrainment is linked to the Dutch scientist, Christian Huygens in 1665. While working on the design of the pendulum clock, Huygens found that when he placed two clocks on a wall near each other and swung the pendulums at different rates, they would eventually end up swinging at the same rate. This is due to their mutual influence on one another. Entrainment can thus be defined as the tendency for two oscillating bodies to lock into phase so that they vibrate in harmony. The principle of entrainment is universal, appearing in chemistry, pharmacology, biology, medicine, psychology, sociology, astronomy, and more. (MS) From wwwdigiserve.com/ gaia.

Fibonacci Numbers: **0, 1, 1, 2, 3, 5, 8, 13** .... (Add the last two to get the next.) This series of numbers is named after Leonardo of Pisa, a mathematician born in Pisa, Italy about 1175 A.D. Leonardo of Pisa called himself Fibonacci, which is short for Filius Bonacci and means "the son of Bonacci." He was a contemporary of another famous Italian—St. Francis of Assisi. The Fibonacci numbers show up in nature in an exquisite spiral pattern, in seashells, in flower petals and seeds, on pineapples, pinecones, and leaf arrangements. The numbers form the basis for the familiar and elegant spiral that we see in the nautilus shell and in the seedhead of the sunflower. (MS) www.mcs. surrey .ac. uk/ personal/ r.knott/ fibonacci.

Ontological Approach to Psychotherapy: Ontology refers to an attempt at understanding a phenomenon by attending to the object and its nature with an optimal degree of specificity. Such observation implies setting aside personal reflections or projections and exercising objectivity in describing data about that which is being observed. Michael Conforti describes this process as the ontological approach. The consequence of such an approach is, he suggests, a move towards understanding manifest form and its emergence or existence due to a stable morphology. This approach moves one to observe how things are present and what informs this process. The advantage of such an approach is that it presses one to look at phenomena within a normative frame rather than focusing on pathology and deviance. (JJ) Assisi Conferences, Seminar on Field, Form, and Fate: Patterns in Mind, Nature and Psyche, 4/7/2001.

Repetition Compulsion: A Freudian term referring to the neurotic, unconscious need to repeat traumatic experiences in order to gain control over them. In Sigmund Freud's *Beyond the Pleasure Principle*, he calls it "compulsion to repeat" (25).

> Enough is left unexplained to justify the hypothesis of a compulsion to repeat—something that seems more primitive, more elementary, more instinctual than the pleasure principle which it over-rides.

Traditionally the term has been understood in that context. However, in the "Assisi" vocabulary it has a broader meaning encompassing the notion that through repetition we maintain the underlying morphology of a system. Extending this point we can say that the function of repetition in the natural world is to insure that the underlying arche-type, morphology, and form will be maintained and preserved in accordance with its own intrinsic design (Conforti, 2001). (MS) Freud, Sigmund (1961). *Beyond the Pleasure Principle.* W. W. Norton, New York, London. Conforti, Michael (2001). Private conversation.

Synchronicity: This term describes events which appear to have an acausal connection which Jung termed "meaningful coincidence." It pertains to the clustering of certain kinds of events and the timing of such clusters which appear to have no connection to time or space and do not appear to be casually related but behave in rela-tionship to each other. (JJ)

> It seems to me synchronicity represents a direct act of cre-ation which manifests itself as chance. The statistical proof of natural conformity to law is therefore only a very lim-ited way of describing nature, since it grasps only uniform events. But nature is essentially discontinuous, i. e., sub-ject to chance. To describe it we need a principle of discontinuity, in psychology this is the drive to individua-tion, in biology it is differentiation, but in nature it is the "meaningful coincidence," that is to say synchronicity. (Jung *CW 18* § 1198).

Unus Mundus: A concept used by Jung to illustrate the unitary nature of the world. Jung suggested that each individual life was interconnected. Jung drew upon the pre-Newtonian idea of a unitary world suggesting that each strata of life is deeply interconnected with every other strata. For instance, the interconnectivity of matter rang-ing from sub-atomic particles to matter on the visible plane in the physical world indicates a fluidity. He also attributed this feature to the operation of the unconscious. (JJ) Samuels, A. (1986). A *Critical Dictionary of Jungian Analysis.* New York: Routledge.

References

Abraham, F., & Gilgen, A. (1995). *Chaos Theory in Psychology.* CT: Prager.

Alexander, C., et el. (1977). *A Pattern Language: Towns, Buildings Construction.* New York: Oxford UP.

Andrews, Alexander. (1989). *Self Organizing Systems. Studies in Cybernetics:* 18. New York: Gordon and Breach.

Bateson, G.H. (1972). *Steps to an Ecology of Mind.* New York: Ballantine.

Bateson, G. H. (1979). *Mind and Nature: A Necessary Unity.* New York: Dutton.

Bateson, W. (1894). *Materials for the Study of Variation.* Boston: Cambridge UP.

Berchulski, S., Conforti, M., Guiter-Mazer, I., and Malone, J. (1987). "Chaotic Attractors in the Therapeutic System." *The Society for Psychoanalytic Psychotherapy Newsletter.* Feb. 1990. Vol 4, No. 1. 10-14. NewYork.

Becker, R. (1990). *Cross Currents: The Perils of Electropollution.* New York: Jeremy Tarcher.

Bohm, David. (1951). *Quantum Theory.* New York. Prentice Hall.

Bohm, David. (1980). *Wholeness and the Implicate Order.* New York: Routledge.

Bohm, David, and B. Hiley. (1975). "On the Intuitive Understanding of Non-Locality as Implied by Quantum Theory." *Foundations of Physics.* 5: 93-109.

Bohm, David, and David F. Peat. (1987). *Science, Order and Creativity: A Dramatic New Look at the Creative Roots of Science and Life.* New York: Bantam.

Calvino, Italo. (1956). *Italian Fairytales.* New York: Harcourt.

Capra, E. (1975). *The Tao of Physics: An Exploration of the Parallels Between Modern Physics and Eastern Mysticism.* Boston: Shambhala.

Card, C. (1991a). "The Archetypal View of C. G. Jung and Wolfgang Pauli. (Part 1)." *Psychological Perspectives.* Spring-Summer. 24: 19-33.

Card, C. (1991b). "The Relevance of the Archetypal Hypothesis to Physics." *Psychological Perspectives.* Fall-Winter. 25: 52-69.

Card, C. (1992). "The Archetypal Hypothesis of Wolfgang Pauli and C. G. Jung: Origins, Development, and Implications." *The Symposium on the Foundations of Modern Physics.* Singapore: World Scientific.

Combs, A. (1996). *The Radiance of Being: Complexity, Chaos and the Evolution of Consciouness.* Edinburgh: Floris.

Conforti, Michael. (1985). "Unconscious Communication in the Initial Interview." Presentation given at the Annual Conference for the Society for Psychoanalytic Psychotherapy. Lenox Hill Hospital, New York.

Conforti, Michael. (1986). "The Externalization of Internal Manic Defense Processes in the Analytic Relationship." Presentation given at the Annual Conference for the Society for Psychoanalytic Psychotherapy. Lenox Hill Hospital, New York.

Conforti, Michael. (1987). "A Phenomenological Study of Patients' Unconscious Responses to the Conditions of Treatment." Diploma Thesis, C. G. Jung Institute, New York.

Conforti, Michael. (1987). "Child Analysis: A Patient's Responses to Disruptions in the Frame." Unpublished article.

Conforti, Michael. (1989). "The Role of Space and Time in the Puer Archetypal Configuration." (Manuscript in preparation for submission for publication.)

Conforti, Michael. (1991). "A Critique of Dr. Theodore Dorpat's Article Entitled: Primary Process Meaning Analysis." *The International Journal of Communicative Psychoanalysis and Psychotherapy.* 7(2): 38-42.

REFERENCES

Conforti, Michael. (1992). "Space and Time in the Cosmos and in Human Experience." Lecture given at the Fourth Annual Assisi, Italy Conference, entitled *The Confluence of Matter and Spirit: The Role of Time, Space and the Emergence of Patterns in the Psyche and Nature.*

Conforti, Michael. (1993). "The Generation of Order and Form Within Archetypal Fields." Lecture given at the Fifth Annual Assisi, Italy Conference, entitled, *The Confluence of Matter and Spirit: Archetypal Fields, Order, and Form.*

Conforti, Michael. (1993). "Evolving Archetypes: Towards a Synthesis of Mind and Universe." Lecture given at the Fifth Annual Assisi, Italy Conference, entitled *The Confluence of Matter and Spirit: Archetypal Fields, Order and Form.*

Conforti, Michael. (1993). "Space and Time in the Cosmos and the Psyche." Lecture given for the Assisi Conference and Seminar Series. June. Woodstock, Vermont.

Conforti, Michael. (1994). "Morphogenetic Dynamics in the Analytic Relationship." *Psychological Perspectives.* Issue 30, Fall-Winter 12-21.

Conforti, M, & Rossi, J. (1998). "Archetypal Dimensions of Territoriality." Unpublished article.

Csanyi, V. (1989). *Evolutionary Systems and Society.* Durham: Duke UP.

Csanyi, V. and G. Kampis. (1985). "Autogenesis: The Evolution of Replicative Systems." *The Journal of Theoretical Biology.* 114: 303-321.

Csanyi, V. and G. Kampis. (1991). "Modelling Biological and Social Change: Dynamical Replicative Network Theory." *The New Evolutionary Paradigm.* Ed. Ervin Laszlo. New York: Gordon and Breach. 77-92.

Davies, P. (1983). *God and the New Physics.* New York: Simon and Schuster.

Davies, P. (1988). *The Cosmic Blueprint: New Discoveries in Nature's Creative Ability to Order the Universe.* New York: Simon & Schuster.

Dorpat, Theodore. (1991). "Primary Process Meaning Analysis." *The Society for Psychoanalytic Psychotherapy Bulletin.* 6(2) 3-11.

Dunn, B. and Jahn, Robert. (1989). "Consciousness, Randomnicity and Information." Ed. Beverly Rubik. Philadephia: Center for Frontier Sciences. 57-82.

Ekeland, I. (1988). *Mathematics and the Unexpected.* Chicago: U of Chicago Press.

Fagg. L. (1999). *Electromagnetism and the Sacred.* New York: Continuum.

Fisher, L. (1907). *Diseases of Infancy and Childhood.* Philadephia: F.A. Davis.

Freud, Sigmund. (1914). "Remembering, Repeating and Working Through." *Standard Edition of the Complete Psychological Works of Sigmund Freud.* Trans. and ed. James Strachey. London: Hogarth. 12: 147-156.

Freud, Sigmund. (1915). "Beyond the Pleasure Principle." *Standard Edition of the Complete Psychological Works of Sigmund Freud.* London: Hogarth. 18: 7-64.

Gamow, G. (1965). *Mr. Tompkins in Paperback.* New York: Cambridge UP.

Giovacchini, J. (1965). "Transference, Incorporation and Synthesis." *Character Disorders and Adaptive Mechanisms.* Ed. P. Giovacchini. New York: Aronson. 263-278.

Giovacchini, J.(1972). "Interpretation and Definition of the Analytic Setting." *Character Disorders and Adaptive Mechanisms.* Ed. P. Giovacchini. New York: Aronson. 367-377.

Giovacchini, J. (1984). *Character Disorders and Adaptive Mechanism.* New York: Jason Aronson.

Goodheart, W. (1984). "C. G. Jung's First Patient: On the Seminal Emergence of Jung's Thought." *Journal of Analytical Psychology.* 29: 1-34.

REFERENCES

Goodwin, B. C. (1972). "Biology and Meaning." *Towards a Theoretical Biology.* London: Edinburgh UP. 259-275.

Goodwin, B. C. (1978). *"A* Cognitive View of Biological Processes." *Journal of Biological Structures.* 1: 117-125.

Goodwin, B. C. (1983). "Organisms and Minds as Dynamic Form." *Leonardo.* Edinburg UP. 22.1: 27-31.

Goodwin, B. C. (1986). *"A* Science of Qualities." *Quantum Implications: Essays in Honor of David Bohm.* Ed. B. J. Hiley and F. David Peat. London: Routledge. 328-337.

Goodwin, B. C. (1989). *Theoretical Biology: Epigenetic and Evolutionary Order from Complex Systems.* Baltimore: Johns Hopkins UP.

Goodwin, B. C. (1989). "Evolution and the Generative Order." *Theoretical Biology: Epigenetic and Evolutionary Order from Complex Systems.* Ed. B. Goodwin and P. Saunders. Baltimore: Johns Hopkins UP. 89-100.

Goodwin, B. C. (1993). "Organisms and Minds as Holistic Dynamic Forms." Lecture given at the Fifth Annual Assisi, Italy Conference, entitled *The Confluence of Matter and Spirit: Archetypal Fields, Order and Form.*

Goodwin, B. C. and Ricard V. Sole. (2002). *Signs of Life: How Complexity Pervades Biology.* New York: Perseus Books.

Gould, Stephen Jay. (1977). *Ontogency and Phylogeny.* Cambridge: Harvard UP.

Gould, Stephen Jay. (1987). "Freud's Phylogenetic Fantasy." *Natural History.* 12: 10-20.

Grotstein, J. (1981). *Splitting and Projective Identification.* New York: Aronson.

Hawking, Stephen. (1988). *A Brief History of Time: From the Big Bang to Black Holes.* New York: Bantam.

Hillman, J. (1996). *The Soul's Code.* New York: Time Warner.

Ho, M.W. (1993). *The Rainbow and the Worm: The Physics of Organisms.* New Jersey: World Scientific.

Ho, M.W. (1998). *Genetic Engineering, Dream or Nightmare: The Brave New World of Bad Science and Big Business.* Michigan: Gateway.

Hunt, V. (1992). "Electromagnetic Properties of Human Mind Field Transactions: The Interaction and Dissolution of Time-Space." Lecture given at the Fourth Annual Assisi, Italy Conference, entitled *The Confluence of Matter and Spirit: The Role of Time, Space and the Emergence of Patterns in the Psyche and Nature.*

Janstch, E. (1980). *The Self Organizing Universe: Scientific and Human Implications of the Emerging Paradigm of Evolution.* New York: Pergamon.

Jensen, R. (1987). "Classical Chaos." *American Scientist.* March-April: 168-181.

Jung, C. G. (1964). *Memories, Dreams and Reflections.* New York: Pantheon.

Jung, C. G. (1968). *Analytical Psychology: Its Theory and Practice.* New York: Random.

Jung, C. G. (1979). *Collected Works of C. G. Jung.* 2nd ed. Trans. R. F. C. Hull. 20 vols. Bollingen Series XX. Princeton: Princeton UP.

Jung, C. G., and Wolfgang Pauli. (1955). *The Interpretations of Nature and the Psyche.* New York: Pantheon.

Kaufmann, Y. (1998). "The Way of the Image." Unpublished article, presented at the 1998 Assisi Conference, Springfield, Vermont.

Keutzer, C. (1982) "Archetypes, Synchronicity and the Theory of Formative Causation." *The Journal of Analytical Psychology.* 27(3): 255-262.

Keutzer, C. (1983). "The 'Theory of Formative Causation' and Its Implication for Archetypes, Parallel Inventions, and the 'Hundredth Monkey' Phenomenon." *Journal of Mind and Behavior.* Summer. 4(3): 353-367.

REFERENCES

Klein, Melanie. (1952). "Notes on Some Schizoid Mechanisms." *Developments in Psychoanalysis.* Ed. M. Klein, R. Heimann, and J. Riviere. London: Hogarth. 292-320.

Klein, Melanie. (1957). "On Identification." *New Directions in Psychoanalysis.* Ed. M. Klein, P. Heiman, and R. Money-Kryle. New York: Basic. 309-345.

Langs, R. (1975). "Therapeutic Misalliances." *The International Journal of Psychoanalytic Psychotherapy.* 4: 77-105.

Langs, R. (1975). "The Therapeutic Relationship and Deviations in Technique." *International Journal of Psychoanalytic Psychotherapy.* 4: 106-141.

Langs, R . (1976). "The Misalliance Dimension in Freud's Case Histories: The Case of Dora." *International Journal of Psychoanalytic Psychotherapy.* 5: 301-317.

Langs, R. (1982). *Psychotherapy: A Basic Text.* New York: Aronson.

Langs, R. (1984). "Making Interpretations and Securing the Frame: A Source of Danger for Psychotherapists." *International Journal of Psychoanalytic Psychotherapy.* New York: Aronson. 10: 3-23.

Langs, R. (1985). "The First Session." *The Yearbook of Psychoanalytic Psychotherapy.* 1: 125-150.

Langs, R. (1986). "A New Model of the Mind." *The Yearbook of Psychoanalysis and Psychotherapy.* 11: 3-31.

Laszlo, Ervin. (1987). *Evolution: The Grand Synthesis.* Boston: Shambhala.

Laszlo, Ervin. (1988). *Evolution: The Cosmic Dimension.* Manuscript.

Laszlo, Ervin. (1990). "Memory in Mind and Nature." Presentation given at the Second Annual Assisi, Italy Conference, Assisi, Italy.

Laszlo, Ervin. (1992). "Unified Fields." Presentation given at the Assisi Conference, Assisi, Italy.

Laszlo, Ervin. (1993). *The Interconnected Universe: Conceptual Foundations of Transdisciplinary Unified Field.* New Jersey: World Scientific.

Laszlo, Ervin. (1994). *The Creative Cosmos. New York: Gordon and Breach.*

Laszlo, Ervin. (1996). "Archetypes, Fields and Dyanmics." Presentation given at the Assisi Conference, Springfield, Vermont.

Mansfield, V. (1995). *Synchronicity, Science and Soul Making.* Chicago: Open Court.

Masson, Jeffrey. (1984). "Freud and the Seduction Theory: A Challenge to the Foundations of Psychoanalysis." *Atlantic Monthly.* February. 33-60.

Maturana, H., & F. Varela. (1980). *Autopoiesis and Cognition: The Realization of the Living.* London: Reidel.

May, Rollo. (1981). *Freedom and Destiny.* New York: Norton.

Meier, C. A. (Ed.) (1992). *Wolfgang Pauli und C. G. Jung, Ein Briefwechsel* 1932-1958. Heielberg: Springer-Verlag.

Mindell, A. (1976). *Synchronicity: An Investigation of the Unitary Background Patterning Synchronous Phenomena.* (*A Psychoid Approach to the Unconscious*). Unpublished Doctoral Dissertation, Union Graduate School.

Neumann, Erich. (1954). *Origins and History of Consciousness.* Princeton: Princeton UP.

Pagels, Heinz. (1982). "Bell's Inequality." *The World of Physics: A Small Library of the Literature of Physics from Antiquity to the Present.* Ed. J. H. Weaver. New York: Simon & Schuster. 11: 160-176.

Peat, F. David. (1987). *Synchronicity: The Bridge Between Mind and Matter.* New York: Bantam.

Peat, F. David. (1988). "Divine Contenders: Wolfgang Pauli and the Symmetry of the World." *Psychological Perspectives.* 19: 14-23.

Peat, F. David. (1997). *Infinite Potential: The Life and Times of David Bohm.* Massachusetts: Adison Wesley.

REFERENCES

Peat, F. David, and J. Briggs. (1989). *The Turbulent Mirror: An Illustrated Guide to Chaos Theory and the Science of Wholeness.* New York: Harper.

Pool, R. (1995). "Catching the Atom Wave." *Science New Series*, Vol. 268. 1129-1130.

Portmann, A. (1964). *New Paths in Biology.* NY: Harper & Row.

Portmann, A. (1972). "Metamorphosis in Animals: The Transformation of The Individual and the Type." In: *Man and Transformation: Papers from the Eranos Yearbooks.* New Jersey: Princeton UP.

Prigogine, I., and I. Stengers. (1984). *Order Out of Chaos: Man's New Dialogue with Nature.* New York: Bantam.

Rapp, P. (1985). "Dynamics of Spontaneous Neural Activity in the Simian Motor Cortex: The Dimension of Chaotic Neurons." *Physics Letters.* 110A. 6: 335-338.

Rapp, P. (1986). "Oscillations and Chaos in Cellular Metabolism and Physiological Systems." *Chaos.* Ed. Λ. V. Holden. Manchester: Manchester UP. 179-208.

Rapp, P., A. Albano, G. deGuzman, and A. I. Mees. (1987). "Data Requirements for Reliable Estimation of Correlation Dimensions." *Chaotic Biological Systems.* Ed. A. V. Holden. New York: Pergamon. 207-220.

Rapp, P., R. A. Latta, and A. I. Mees. (1988). "Parameter-Dependent Transitions and the Optimal Control of Dynamical Diseases." *Bulletin of Mathematical Biology.* 50.3: 227-253.

Reik, T. (1954). *Listening With the Third Ear.* New York: Farrar, Straus & Giroux.

Ritsema, R. (2003). "The Periplus of the Eranos Archetype." Unpublished article.

Rosen, R. (1987). "Some Epistemological Issues in Physics and Biology." *Quantum Implications: Essays in Honor of David Bohm.* Ed. B. J. Hiley and F. David Peat. New York: Routledge. 314-327.

Schmeck, H. (1974). *Immunity: The Double Edged Sword.* New York: Braziller.

Sheldrake, Rupert. (1981). *A New Science of Life: The Hypothesis of Formative Causation.* Boston: Houghton & Mifflin.

Sheldrake, Rupert (1987). "Mind, Memory and Archetype." *Psychological Perspectives.* Vol: 18(1) 9-25.

Sheldrake, Rupert. (1988). *The Presence of the Past.* London: Collins.

Sperry, R. W. (1951). "Mechanisms of Neural Maturation." *Handbook of Experimental Psychology.* Ed. S. Stevens. London: Wiley. 236-281.

Sperry, R. W. (1956). "The Eye and the Brain." *Scientific American.* May. 48-52.

Thom, R. (1972). *Structural Stability and Morphogenesis.* Reading, PA: Benjamin.

Thom, R. (1989). "An Inventory of Waddingtonian Concepts." *Theoretical Biology: Epigenetic and Evolutionary Order from Complex Systems.* Ed. B. Goodwin and R. Saunders. 1-7.

Voofiles, W. (1996). *Nature.* March 21, 1996.

Von Franz, M.-L. (1980). *On Divination and Synchronicity.* Toronto: Inner City.

Von Franz, M.-L. (1992). *Psyche and Matter.* Boston: Shambhala.

Von Franz, M.-L. (1993). *Puer Aeternus: A Psychological Study of the Adult Struggle with the Paradise of Childhood.* 2nd ed. n. p.: Sigo.

Von Franz, M.-L. (1997). *Archetypal Patterns in Fairy Tales.* Toronto: Inner City.

Waddington, C. H. (Ed.) (1972). *Towards a Theoretical Biology: 4 Essays.* Edinburgh: Edinburgh UP.

REFERENCES

Weinberg, S. (1978). *The First Three Minutes*. New York: Fontana.

Weaver, J. (1987). "The Einstein Universe and the Bohr Atom." *The World of Physics: A Small Library of the Literature of Physics from Antiquity to the Present. Vol 11*. New York: Simon and Schuster. 313-338.

Whitehead, Alfred North. (1978). *Process and Reality*. New York: Free Press.

Whitmont, E. (1966). "The Destiny Concept in Psychotherapy." *The Analytic Process: Aims, Analysis, Training: The Proceedings of The Fourth International Congress for Analytical Psychology*. Ed. Joseph Wheelwright. New York: Putnam. 185-198.

Wilson, E. O. (1998). *Consilience: The Unity of Knowledge*. New York: Knopf.

Winnicott, D. W. (1935). "The Manic Defense." *Through Pediatrics to Psychoanalysis*. Ed. D. W. Winnicott. New York: Basic. 129-145.

Zukav, Gary. (1979). *The Dancing Wu Li Masters: An Overview of the New Physics*. New York: Quill.

Index

About the Author

Michael Conforti, Ph.D. is the Founder and Director of the Assisi Conferences and Seminars, and is considered a pioneer in the field of Matter-Psyche Studies. He is a Jungian Analyst and faculty member at the C.G. Jung Institute-Boston, The C.G. Jung Foundation – New York, and author of *Field, Form and Fate: Patterns in Mind, Nature and Psyche*. Dr. Conforti lectures in the United States and abroad including Italy, Denmark, the Caribbean, Venezuela and the C.G. Jung Institute – Zurich.

The Assisi Conferences and Seminars investigate the interface between Jungian psychology and the "new sciences". They are recognized as an international focal point for examining the influence of archtypal processes in the individual and collective psyche, the therapeutic situation and other areas of the natural world.

The Two-Year Certificate Program offers participants the opportunity to engage in an in-depth ongoing study of Jungian psychology and the "new sciences". These areas of specialized training include archetypal pattern recognition, archetypal field theory, self-organization and inherent ordering processes in the personal and collective psyche.

Organizational Consultation, Training and Mentoring Dr. Conforti and the faculty of the Assisi Conferences offer training, consultation and mentoring to help organizations and executives to identify the archetypal patterns which influence their businesses. This work involves archetypal pattern recognition and the implementation of interventions, which help move these systems towards a more generative alignment.

For additional information about these programs contact:
> **Assisi Conferences and Seminars**
> **Post Office Box 6033**
> **Brattleboro, VT 05302**
> **(802) 254-6220**
> *www.assisiconferences.com*